GOD *and* EVIL

GOD *and* EVIL

by

H. J. McCLOSKEY

MARTINUS NIJHOFF / THE HAGUE / 1974

DEDICATION

To Mary A.

Without whom this book would neither have been conceived of, nor embarked upon, nor completed.

ISBN 90 247 1604 7

PRINTED IN THE NETHERLANDS

ACKNOWLEDGEMENTS

This book results from reflection over a number of years concerning the problem of evil. During the past three years I have been fortunate enough to have had frequent discussions with Father M. B. Ahern, and, although the conclusions towards which this book is directed are such that he would reject certain of them, it is greatly indebted to him and to these discussions. I wish also to express my great appreciation of the many thoughtful comments and criticisms Father Ahern made concerning the final draft of this work. I have not acted on them all. The book may be the worse for this.

I must also thank my friends, Professor D. M. Armstrong of the University of Sydney, Mr. Lauchlan Chipman and Mr. Wayne Stuart of the University of Melbourne, Mr. F. C. Jackson and Mr. N. Szorenyi-Reischl of La Trobe University, all of whom have read the final draft of this work and suggested various amendments. I have acted on many but by no means all of these suggestions. The responsibility for any shortcomings the book has, remains entirely mine. Most especially I thank my wife, Dr. Mary A. McCloskey of the University of Melbourne, for her help and encouragement at all stages of this book.

In this work I have drawn on material from three of my articles. I wish to thank the editor of the *Philosophical Quarterly* for permission to make use of material from "God and Evil" which appeared in Volume 10, 1960; the editor of the *Journal of Bible and Religion* (now the *Journal of the American Academy of Religion*) for my use of material from "The Problem of Evil" which appeared in Volume XXX, 1962; and finally I thank also the editor of the *Southern Journal of Philosophy* for the use I make of "Would Any Being Merit Worship?", from Volume 2, 1964, of that Journal.

H. J. McCloskey
1972

TABLE OF CONTENTS

CHAPTER I

THE PROBLEM STATED:
THE NEED FOR A SOLUTION

Traditionally, the problem of evil has been seen to arise from the apparent self-contradiction involved in asserting that God, an all-perfect Creator exists, and that evil exists. The problem has been set out over the centuries in many, including the following ways:

"Epicurus' old questions are yet unanswered.

Is he willing to prevent evil, but not able? then is he impotent. Is he able, but not willing? then is he malevolent. Is he both able and willing? whence then is evil?" [1]

Lactantius, also reporting Epicurus, stated the problem thus:

"God either wishes to take away evils, and is unable; or He is able, and is unwilling; or He is neither willing nor able, or He is both willing and able. If He is willing and is unable, He is feeble, which is not in accordance with the character of God; if He is able and unwilling, He is envious, which is equally at variance with God; if He is neither willing nor able, He is both envious and feeble, and therefore not God; if He is both willing and able, which alone is suitable to God, from what source then are evils? or why does He not remove them?" [2]

St. Augustine is commonly attributed the formulation: "Either God cannot abolish evil or he will not; if he cannot, he is not all-powerful; if he will not, he is not all-good."

Boethius presented the problem briefly as:

"If there be a God, from whence proceed so many evils?" [3]

St. Thomas Aquinas presented the problem in the following way:

"It seems that God does not exist; because if one of two contraries be infinite, the other would be altogether destroyed. But the name of God means that He is infinite goodness. If, therefore, God existed, there would

---

[1] D. Hume, *Dialogues Concerning Natural Religion*, Pt. X.

[2] *The Works of Lactantius*, (*On the Anger of God*, ch. 13, trans. W. Fletcher), Edinburgh, T. & T. Clark, 1871.

[3] *De Consolatione Philosophiae*, Bk. 1, sn. iv.

be no evil discoverable; but there is evil in the world. Therefore God does not exist. Further, it is superfluous to suppose that what can be accounted for by a few principles has been produced by many. But it seems that everything we see in the world can be accounted for by other principles, supposing God did not exist. For all natural things can be reduced to one principle, which is human reason, or will. Therefore, there is no need to suppose God's existence." [4]

G. H. Joyce set out the problem as follows:

"The existence of evil in the world must at all times be the greatest of all problems which the mind encounters when it reflects on God and his relation to the world. If He is, indeed, all-good and all-powerful, how has evil any place in the world which He has made? Whence came it? Why is it here? If He is all-good why did He allow it to arise? If all-powerful, why does He not deliver us from the burden? Alike in the physical and moral order creation seems so grievously marred that we find it hard to understand how it can derive in its entirety from God." [5]

C. Journet asks and observes:

"If God does not exist, where does good come from? If he does exist, where does evil come from? If God is the source of good, can he also be the source of evil? . . .

Evil exists and God exists. Their coexistence is a mystery." [6]

More recently, J. L. Mackie and A. Flew have argued against the existence of God from the problem of evil, setting out the problem in the following ways:

"God is omnipotent; God is wholly good; yet evil exists. There seems to be some contradiction between these three propositions, so that if any two of them were true the third would be false. But at the same time all three are essential parts of most theological positions." [7]

"The issue is whether to assert at the same time first that there is an infinitely good God, second that he is an all-powerful Creator, and third that there are evils in his universe, is to contradict yourself." [8]

Elsewhere I have set out the problem observing:

---

[4] *Summa Theologiae* (*Summa Theologica,* trans. by the Dominican Fathers – all subsequent quotations from this work are from this translation), 1, 2, art. 3, obj. 1, 2.
[5] *Principles of Natural Theology,* London, Longmans, Green and Co., 3rd edition, 1923, New Impression, 1957, p. 583.
[6] *The Meaning of Evil,* London, Geoffrey Chapman, 1963. Translated by Michael Barry, p. 58.
[7] J. L. Mackie, "Evil and Omnipotence", *Mind,* LXIV, 1955, p. 200.
[8] A. Flew, *God and Philosophy,* London, Hutchinson, 1966, p. 48.

"The problem of evil is a very simple problem to state. There is evil in the world; yet the world is said to be the creation of a good, omnipotent God. How is this possible? Surely a good, omnipotent being would have made a world that is free of evil of any kind." [9]

These various statements suggest that the problem of evil is that of showing that no *self-contradiction* is involved in jointly asserting that an all-perfect God exists and that some/any evil exists. This is how the problem has traditionally been represented. One painful pin prick, one toothache, one act of cruelty, or one minor, selfish act of dishonesty would be sufficient to give rise to the problem of evil as it has traditionally been conceived of and explained, namely as that of reconciling God's omnipotence, omniscience (which can be interpreted as being involved in his omnipotence), and perfect goodness, with the existence of *any* evil at all in the world. In fact, even in traditional discussions the problem of evil is not one problem only, but a number of distinct problems which need to be distinguished. Those who have stated the problem in the above ways, in terms of the problem posed by any evil at all, have often gone on to offer solutions to the very significantly different problem, namely, that posed by the actual evil which occurs, i.e. the kinds and amount of actual evil. Others have seen the problem of evil in other ways, for instance, as one internal to religion (consider Journet's statement above), or as that concerning whether a belief in God in the light of any or actual evil can be shown to be rational, or at least not irrational, where rational and irrational need not refer to the absence or presence of a logical self-contradiction. Consider here Hick's statements:

"For us today the live question is whether this (evil) renders impossible a rational belief in God." [10]

"The aim of a Christian theodicy must thus be the relatively modest and defensive one of showing that the mystery of evil, largely incomprehensible though it remains, does not render irrational a faith that has arisen, not from inferences of natural theology, but from participation in a stream of religious experience which is continuous with that recorded in the Bible." [11]

It is therefore of vital importance that the various distinct problems of evil be distinguished at the outset of our discussion. For convenience of reference in later discussions, the various problems may be distinguished in the following ways.

Traditional Problem of Evil 1. This is the problem posed by the exist-

---

[9] "The Problem of Evil", *Journal of Bible and Religion*, XXX, 1962, p. 187.
[10] J. Hick, *Evil and the God of Love*, London, Macmillan, 1966, p. 280.
[11] *Ibid.*, p. 281.

ence of any evil at all. It is the problem of showing that the apparent logical contradiction involved in asserting that God, an all-perfect being possessing the attributes of omnipotence, omniscience, and all goodness, created the world, and that the world contains evil, is not a real contradiction. This problem would be resolved if it is shown that the existence of *some* evil is compatible with divine perfection.[12]

Traditional Problem of Evil 2. In seeking to offer solutions to this Problem 1, theists have usually moved on to advance solutions to the very different problem of evil, namely that posed by the existence of the actual evil which occurs in the world. Others, including C. A. Campbell, whilst not dismissing Problem 1 as simply a pseudo-problem, regard this Problem 2 as the really serious problem, Campbell observing:

"What does disquiet us is the occurrence of undeserved suffering that is both immoderate in degree – sometimes excruciating – and also long protracted." [13]

Actual evil, with its various kinds and amounts, poses a logical problem in the sense that again there is an apparent logical contradiction involved in asserting that this world is the creation of an all-powerful, all-knowing, all-good, all-perfect being, and that it contains such evil as it does. Solutions to this problem must involve reference to the kinds and amounts of evil – moral evils, human and animal suffering, human and animal pains.

Traditional Problem of Evil 3. The foregoing two problems are problems which arise from there being an apparent contradiction in asserting that God exists, and that evil (some or certain kinds and amounts) exists. There is a third, distinct problem which is often confused with these two problems, concerning the compatibility of evil which occurs with God's perfection as an all-powerful, all-knowing, all-good being. Here the problem is not a problem of logical compatibility, it is not a problem which proceeds on the basis that for there to be a problem there must be an apparent logical contradiction, but rather it is a problem which arises from the apparent *moral incompatibility* of the claims that God, an all-perfect being, created the world, and that the world contains the evil it does. The incompatibility may be claimed to be one which springs from the impossibility of an all-perfect being creating or allowing such evil, where the impossibility relates to synthetic necessary truths and impossibilities. Many discussions of the

---

[12] In spite of the importance traditionally and currently attached to this problem, by theists and atheists alike, E. H. Madden and P. H. Hare in *Evil and the Concept of God* (Springfield, Charles C. Thomas, 1968) dismiss it in a sentence as a sterile problem in favour of Problem 2.

[13] *On Selfhood and Godhood,* London, Allen & Unwin, 1957, p. 288.

problem of evil are such as to be directed at showing that this kind of incompatibility does or does not result from the evil actually to be found in the world.

Problem of Evil 4. A further, distinct problem of evil, parallel to the traditional Problem 2, will be noted and discussed briefly in Chapter 5. This is the problem of the logical compatibility of the evil which actually occurs and the claim that a finite God, who is explained as the creator of this world and as being either all-powerful and of limited goodness, or as of finite power and wholly good, or as being possessed of specified degrees of power and goodness, exists. Here too, apparent contradictions may arise, more obviously in respect of the second than of the first or third alternatives.

Problem of Evil 5. Parallel to Problem 3, a problem concerning the compatibility of the claim that a finite creator of the universe who possesses the attributes of complete power and limited, determinate goodness, or limited determinate power and complete goodness, or limited determinate power and goodness, exists, with the acknowledgement of the existence of the evil which actually occurs, arises also where the compatibility or incompatibility is explained in terms other than that of logical compatibility or logical contradiction, i.e. as moral compatibility or incompatibility.

There are variations on the above problems, and problems in addition to them which arise for the theist from the possibility or actuality of evil. As noted above, Journet and Hick both see the problem confronting the theist as that of explaining the existence of any and actual evil within the framework of Christian belief – in the case of the former in terms of traditional Christian belief, with the latter in terms of a skilful, ingenious, although at times clumsy mixing of traditional and novel Christian beliefs. The theist's problem also admits of being interpreted as one in terms of probabilities, namely, whether the considerations, evidence, arguments, relevant thereto, are such as to create a greater or lesser probability in favour of a belief that a contradiction is involved in asserting that God created the world and that some or actual evil exists, or in favour of a claim that the existence of God and evil are in some other way incompatible and irreconcilable. If the considerations in favour of there being no contradiction or incompatibility are greater, then the claim that both God and evil exist is irrational, would obviously be weakened or undermined; and *vice versa.*

The Logical Problems. Ever since the problem of evil has seriously been considered, it has been noted that in order to show that there is a logical contradiction involved in asserting that an all-perfect creator (one who is omnipotent, omniscient, and all good) exists, and that evil (some, or the actual kinds and amount) exists, an ethical connecting link needs to be supplied to bring out the precise nature of the self-contradiction involved in the joint assertion. The connecting link must be an analytic, ethical principle if the contradiction or incompatibility that is claimed to exist, is to be a logical one involving a self-contradiction. As M. B. Ahern and A. Plantinga have argued, philosophers have not been as evidently successful as theists and atheists have been inclined to suppose in setting out plausible, connecting links of the kind needed to show that the traditional Problem of Evil 1 is a *prima facie* or a real problem. Typically, synthetic propositions have been advanced as the connecting link, and the propositions so advanced have been false propositions.

M. B. Ahern, after noting:

"It is easy to supply analytically true principles about power and many philosophers have done so, e.g.:

Epicurus: A being which is willing to take away evils and is unable, is feeble.

Hume: A being willing to prevent evil but not able is impotent.

J. L. Mackie: There are no limits to what an omnipotent being can do." [14]

Goes on to argue that this is not so in respect of principles concerning goodness. Here he argues:

"Principles about goodness used by Epicurus, Augustine, Hume, Mackie and R. D. Bradley will now be studied. First it will be asked whether they are analytically true. If they are not, it will then be asked whether they are satisfactory when reformulated as analytically true principles.

Epicurus, Augustine and Hume use principles sufficiently similar to be taken together:

Epicurus: A being which is able to take away evil and unwilling to do so is malicious.

Augustine: A being which will not abolish evil when it can is not all good.

Hume: A being which is able but not willing to prevent evil is malevolent.

Since the general problem of evil concerns not merely the removing of existing evil but the preventing of every evil, Hume's principle is to be preferred to the other two.

[14] M. B. Ahern, *The Problem of Evil*, London, Routledge & Kegan Paul, 1971, p. 34.

It does not seem possible to make out even a *prima facie* case that Hume's principle is analytically true." [15]

Ahern then goes on to note that the non-prevention of both moral and non-moral evil may be morally justified, and that any restatement of the ethical principle which takes note of this, for example, "A being which is able but not willing to prevent evil is malevolent, unless it is justified in not preventing the evil" [16] or that of Mackie "Good is opposed to evil in such a way that a good thing always eliminates evil as far as it can" [17] can no longer be used to show that the traditional Problem 1, which relates to *any* evil, is even a *prima facie* problem.

A. Plantinga in *God and Other Minds* had made the same point in respect of Mackie's and my discussions of the problem. He noted of Mackie's discussion that:

"Mackie, however, recognizes that 'the contradiction does not arise immediately; to show it we need some additional premises, or perhaps some quasi-logical rules connecting the terms 'good', 'evil', and 'omnipotent'. These additional premises are that 'good is opposed to evil, in such a way that a good thing always eliminates evil as far as it can, and that there are no limits to what an omnipotent thing can do'." [18]

Plantinga then goes on to bring out the difficulties in the way of Mackie and others making the ethical connecting link more precise. As will be evident in the subsequent discussion in this work, Plantinga and Ahern have raised an issue of major importance. Implicit in many traditional discussions of the traditional Problem 1 is some such principle as that set out by Plato in the *Republic,* Book III, 380, namely that a wholly good being (God) cannot be the source of evil. Examples drawn from the human situation easily reveal difficulties for such a principle in respect of finite beings, less evidently as we shall see in respect of an all-powerful being. Similar difficulties arise in respect of principles stated or assumed by those who have accepted the problem as a crucial one for theism. Yet, even were it to be shown that no analytic principle had yet been set out which provides the connecting link, this would not establish that there is no such analytic connecting link to be found. Further, it is possible to state what is as relevant and adequate as such a principle here, namely, that an all-perfect being will always choose the world which is better than a world which is less good, and in particular, a world which is better and contains

---

[15] *Op. cit.,* pp. 34-5.
[16] *Ibid.,* p. 35.
[17] *Ibid.,* p. 36.
[18] *God and Other Minds,* Ithaca, Cornell, 1967, p. 121.

less evil, than a world which is less good and contains more evil. Unless it is argued that God's creative powers are limited and that a Leibnizian notion of the best possible world is a coherent one and such that such a world *must* contain evil (and this will later be denied) then it would seem analytically to follow from God's omnipotence and goodness that he can make a world that is wholly good and which is better than a world containing evil; that it is true of any specific or specifiable determinate universe containing *any* evil. To argue otherwise is to limit God's power by allowing that he *must* allow, cause, or permit evil to make a world which is better than one which is wholly good; and since there will be a possible wholly good world better than the former, the problem breaks out again. This however is to anticipate a later discussion.

Although most discussions of the problem of evil start out from a statement of Problem 1, they usually very quickly move on to considering Problem 2, with solutions to that problem being advanced. The move from the one problem to the other usually takes the form of inserting some such connecting link as 'An omnipotent, wholly good God would neither create nor permit avoidable, unnecessary, unjustified, or undeserved evils'. Here it is argued by some that the principles in terms of avoidable and undeserved evils are neither analytic nor true, that avoidable and undeserved evils may be justified in terms of goods to which they give rise. On the other hand, whilst the principles in terms of unnecessary and unjustified evils are analytic, they are such as to focus the problem on the actual evil which has occurred, will occur, and is occurring, its kinds and amounts. Similar analytic connecting links may be set out in respect of the various possible logical problems noted as Problem 4. For example, a wholly good finite God would not permit unnecessary, avoidable, unjustified evils. Again the problem becomes one concerning actual evils, in this case of the all-good finite God, as to whether the evil which is to be found in the world is unnecessary, avoidable, and unjustified. In the case of the God of finite goodness, the issue would relate to whether the amount of evil was disproportionate to his goodness/evilness.

Problems of Evil not involving logical contradictions. Problems 3 and 5 are explained as resulting from an apparent incompatibility between claims that God, defined in 3 as all-perfect, or in 5 as finite, exists, and that evil may exist or exists, where the incompatibility is not one involving a self-contradiction but is of another kind, for instance, a moral one. To illustrate: The assertion 'A wholly good person or being always does what he ought' is analytic, whereas 'A wholly good being always lessens the general happiness, or always breaks his promises, or always lies' are synthetic (and false). To assert that 'A always does what he ought' and also 'A always lessens the general happiness when he can, or always breaks his promises, or always lies' is not to contradict oneself. However I wish to argue that the latter are incompatible assertions which can be shown to be such by reference to non-analytic ethical principles. This kind of incompatibility is as serious as logical incompatibility. In so far as it appears to arise in respect of God and any or actual evil, to that extent there are problems that the theist must show to be only apparent and not real. Consider the example 'X inflicts excruciating pain and suffering on his children daily', 'X is wholly good'. There is an obvious incompatibility between such statements, yet the incompatibility is not due to some such principle as 'A wholly good man would not cause his children excruciating pain and suffering' being analytically true – it is not analytic and its truth is a matter open to dispute. None the less, whether X is explained as being Bill Smith or God, there is an apparent, *prima facie* incompatibility between the assertions which demands to be shown not to be a real incompatibility, if both assertions are to be accepted as true. This point rests on the fact that the good man is he who acts on the true principles of morality (analytic), whilst the true principles are synthetic, not analytic truths. They are, as I have argued elsewhere, synthetic *a priori* truths.[19]

In this work, therefore, I shall be concerned with a number of problems and not simply with one of the traditional problems of evil. Where possible, I shall take up the challenge thrown out by Plantinga who argued:

"What McCloskey must show is that it is *logically impossible* that there is evil and that all of it is justified; if it is even possible that all evil is justified, then, surely, there is no contradiction in the joint assertion of (a) - (e)." [20]

However this is only part of the group of problems known as the problem of evil, and subsequent discussion will relate to the variety of problems noted above.

ON THE NEED FOR SOLUTIONS TO THE PROBLEM OF EVIL

It is not uncommonly suggested by theists that the problem of evil is not such a serious problem as it may at first seem to be, as there are satisfactory grounds for belief in God, for example from the proofs, faith, religious experience, miracles, and that as against such positive grounds for belief in God, the problem of evil must constitute only a *prima facie* and not a

---

[19] *Meta-Ethics and Normative Ethics,* The Hague, Martinus Nijhoff, 1969.
[20] *Op. cit.,* p. 123.

real difficnlty for theism, and be more a problem within theism, namely that of reconciling what we know to be true, than that of determining what is true in respect of the nature, attributes and existence of God. Th'is the problem of evil is sometimes explained as that of gaining understanding about the coexistence of God and evil and hence not as one which raises the question of God's existence. It is concerning this rather complacent view that I wish to raise some queries, and to suggest that the problem of evil raises in a very real way the whole issue of God's existence. My line of argument here is that the important proofs, and the beliefs which spring from faith, religious experience, miracles, and other like considerations, are challenged or qualified by the fact of evil. Here I shall disregard the ontological proof, it being immune from this contention, for the twofold reasons, that there appear to be impressive objections which may be urged against it and because I do not believe that anyone has ever become a serious, convinced theist as a result of being persuaded of the cogency of the ontological argument.

The cosmological argument may be set out in various ways, and is not, as the name suggests, one argument, but several. It may be developed as an argument from the existence of something, as an argument from the exist-ence of this world, and as either an argument to a first cause or to a suffi-cient reason. As an argument from the existence of something to the exist-ence of a necessary (non-dependent) first cause, to the existence of an all-perfect being, it involves a conceptual move from the notion of a necessary being to that of an all-perfect being. How else is it shown that the necessary first cause is all-perfect? The conceptual move is akin to that in the onto-logical argument but lacks even the apparent plausibility of that move. One might well ask here what the conceptual reasons for this move are. If there are no good conceptual reasons, the proof fails to provide a conclusion which renders the problem of evil an unreal problem. If the argument from the existence of the world is to be different from this, it can only be because it takes note of the features of the world, its magnitude, change, and the like. In that event, it must move to a first cause which is account-able for the evil as well as for the good, and also for the immensity of the universe. This would seem to create an initial difficulty in the way of mov-ing from a necessary first cause to an all-perfect first cause. If the necessar-y first cause created the evil in the world, or even allowed or permitted it, the question must arise as to how it can be all-perfect. Any purely con-ceptual argument to a first cause must take note of evil as part of the effect of the creative activities of this first cause. This would seem to involve meeting the problem of evil in the process, and hence is no reason for dismissing the problem as one for which there *must* be a solution although we may not know what it is. The argument from "Something exists, to a sufficient reason, to a necessary being, to God", involves the doubt as to whether an all-perfect God must be postulated as the only possible sufficient reason, and further encounters special difficulty because of the nature of the world with the actual evil which is to be found in it, and for which the sufficient reason is such. To postulate an all-perfect sufficient reason in the light of the fact of evil is to beg the question.

The teleological argument and the argument from design are no more satisfactory, and for much the same reasons. One cannot legitimately argue, as do exponents of these arguments, from there being some sort of evidence of purpose or design to there being an all-powerful, all-perfect planner or designer. In the face of the existence of evil, this is to beg the question. It might be suggested that the teleological argument really involves an unstated conceptual or *a priori* move which makes the fact of evil irrelevant. This might well be true. Certainly the argument requires the inclusion of further steps to establish the existence of a first cause, and of a perfect first cause. However, we can know whether this is so only if the conceptual or *a priori* moves are laid bare. In this context, it is significant that theists who invoke these arguments usually also concern themselves with the problem of evil as a real problem, and as one which raises the question of the existence of God, and not as one concerning what the, at present time unknown, solution might be. It has been suggested that what has been said concerning these arguments is true of the argument from design but not of the teleological argument, where the latter is construed as an argument from evidence of purpose. It is undoubtedly true that the latter encounters less evident difficulty from the fact of evil than the former, but it still encounters serious difficulty. Here it might be asked, how, from the partial evidence of purpose – conceivably perfect, conceivably very imperfect – it can be concluded that an all-perfect God exists. These considerations bring out another feature of these arguments, namely that they are at most arguments from probability and not apodeitic as claimed, and as such leave the theist open to the various problems posed by the fact of evil. At best they would show that there is some probability that God exists. Evil would then be a ground for questioning this probability judgment.

Many theists come to their belief in God in other ways, for example, though faith. Tillich spoke of faith as the state of being ultimately concerned, as claiming truth for its concern, and as involving commitment, courage, and the taking of a risk.[21] This issue will be discussed in more detail in Chapter 8, Section A, (ix), where it will be argued that to have faith in the existence of a wholly perfect God in the face of the existence and reality of evil is indeed to take a risk, a risk that is not rationally justified.

It is sufficient also to note here that awareness and experience of evil are equally relevant to religious experience and what can be concluded from religious experience. Similarly, what conclusions can be drawn from miracles, must be qualified by the fact of evil. In any case, there are many other telling considerations against basing a belief in the existence of an all-perfect God on such grounds.

In suggesting that there are weaknesses in the conclusions based on such considerations as have been touched on above, I have simply been concerned *to suggest* that the fact of the existence of evil may constitute a problem for the theist who reflects about the adequacy of these grounds for a belief in the existence of an all-perfect God, in the light of the fact of evil. Whether or not it is the case that the existence of evil can or cannot provide conclusive grounds for disbelief in the existence of an all perfect being, this fact concerning the relevance of evil to the question of the adequacy of the more common grounds of belief in God is of importance. The possible arguments for the existence of God are unlimited in number, hence until all possible arguments are refuted, and until it is shown that any (some) or actual evil is logically incompatible with the existence of God, it will remain possible that both propositions: God exists; Evil exists: will be true. For this reason much of this work will be aimed at indicating the direction in which the weight of evidence points.

[21] Paul Tillich, *The Dynamics of Faith*, London, Allen & Unwin, 1957.

CHAPTER II

EVILS: PAST, PRESENT AND FUTURE

The evils that call for explanation and justification are of various kinds which it is important to distinguish when considering all the problems other than Problem 1 noted in the previous Chapter. One of the most significant features of most kinds of evils that occur is that far from arising from chance happenings they result from inbuilt features of our world.

Firstly, there is the pain and suffering of animals, children, and adult human beings, that is, of some beings who are helpless and who can do nothing or little to lessen their suffering, and of others who sometimes but more usually not, bring their sufferings upon themselves. The evils involved include *privations* so-called, such as blindness, deafness, *insanity,* inbecility and senility, with the consequent pain and suffering these privations bring in their wake. Related to these privations is *the manner of degeneration and ageing* of sentient beings – the growing helplessness, the condition politely referred to as "senility", and the evils to which it exposes the aged. What appears to be the natural mode of ageing and *dying* in animals and men is one which brings hurt, suffering, and, in human beings, very often humiliation and broken spirits. The lot of the aged is a sad, lonely one, and often a quite wretched one. It is evidently much worse in most societies other than that in which I live, and this, very often, is due to no moral fault of the members of the society concerned but to environmental factors and the economic level of development they allow the society to attain.

The evils in the world which call for explanation include other *natural processes* besides ageing and dying, most notably that of child-bearing with the suffering and indeed the misery it may involve, and which often, even typically, it did involve before the use of anaesthetics and control of disease of the kind we have today. Further, there is *the evil of the existence of beings who live and who can only live by preying on others, hurtfully killing them in their efforts to survive.* The fact that the universe contains creatures such as carnivors, and, for that matter, meat-eating beings such as ourselves, beings who can sustain themselves only by killing, sometimes only in unavoidably cruel ways, harmless sentient beings, is an imperfection which calls for explanation and justification. A world free of such an evil, one which would not involve the existence of orders or kinds of beings such that some were obliged to kill, painfully to kill, others, or themselves agonizingly albeit "heroically" to starve to death, would seem to be a world more in keeping with what we should expect of a perfect creator. Many parasites come into this general category, living on and at the same time hurtfully harming the hosts on whom they live. The worst such organisms in this respect, and these include but are not restricted to parasitic organisms, are disease organisms.

Disease, even more than the natural disorders or diseases of degeneration and ageing, causes vast pain and suffering both to its victims and to their loved ones and to those dependent on them. It may be that the time will come with the advance of medicine on the one hand, and the development of human technology on the other, that wars and machines such as cars will cause more suffering. That time has not yet arrived. Whether or not it will ever arrive is unimportant. What is important is that diseases cause and have caused a vast amount of suffering. A number of points need to be made here. Firstly, it is true and important that great advances have been made in the way of prevention and treatment of diseases, and much has been achieved by way of lessening the effects of many diseases. The development of anaesthetics has greatly reduced the pain involved in the treatment of various diseases. The development of artificial limbs has reduced both the pain and suffering to which those lacking limbs are exposed. Also many diseases can today be prevented, controlled, or have their effects lessened. Consider here diseases such as poliomyelitis, diphtheria, cholera, yellow fever, the bubonic plague, tetanus, and how they may be checked or prevented by vaccination. Consider too the preventative measures which may be taken against malaria, tuberculosis, cancer, and other major diseases, and the great advances that have occurred in the treatment of many diseases, including the above and the other "killer" diseases of former times such as pneumonia, scarlet fever, and the like. Great advances are being made in lessening the effects of many diseases and in preventing the occurrence of others. However, even if by the end of this decade or this century, medical science so advanced that every pain could be prevented and every disease eliminated, those pains and those diseases, together with the sufferings they caused, would remain a source of a problem which required explanation and justification. Secondly it is important to note the vast variety of diseases, with their range of unpleasant symptoms and effects, and the very considerable variety of painful results, the pains varying in quality, duration, intensity, and the like. It is tempting, when considering the variety of pains and forms of suffering, to conclude that the world is a creation of a clever sadist, who addressed himself to the problem of devising a complex system of pains and sufferings, and of diseases which involve them. Some diseases bring loss of faculties and great distress – consider paralyzing strokes which leave the victim conscious but incapable of speech, or diseases such as brain tumours, which bring great pain and even blindness before ultimate death. Some diseases bring very distressing but not permanently harmful symptoms, for example, boils over the body, varieties of dermatitis, and the like. Other diseases strike suddenly and with intense pain which continues sometimes for years, sometimes for only a short time until the disease kills off its possessor. Some give warning of what is to come, giving the victim time to worry and to suffer anxiety without the hope of relief or cure, others also bring gradual degeneration of the body and mind as with leprosy in former times, and with many diseases including multiple sclerosis and syphilis. Some hold the suffering person in suspense, as with meningitis and encephalitis, when only time tells whether grave effects will result from the disease. Some diseases come to their victims even before they are born as with syphilis which the child receives from its mother, or as with hydrocephalus, congenital blindness, idiocy, and many other unwanted conditions including deformities and lack of organs and limbs.

The variety of diseases and the variety of harm they cause, the variety of pains and the variety of distresses and misery they cause, are immense. Further, some diseases may advance to the incurable state without revealing their presence, even where they are of the kind of disease which admits of full cure when diagnosed in the early stages. They include diseases which ultimately involve suffering which brings with it no evident good to many of its victims, but often moral degeneration, and to the victim's loved ones, misery. Again, as already noted, various diseases may come to totally innocent children before birth, and in certain cases, be certain to do so even at the moment of conception. Disease therefore poses a real problem for the theist. One would not expect to find the vast range and variety of diseases with their painful effects in a world claimed to be created by an all-perfect, omnipotent, omniscient, all-good being.

The occurrence in the universe of *natural phenomena which bring pain and suffering to men and animals* also calls for explanation. The phenomena of avalanches, landslides, earthquakes, volcanoes, tidal waves, floods, droughts, and the like, are evils in that they cause immense suffering, suffering that those involved could not have avoided without superhuman foresight and powers. It is probably true today that an egalitarian distribution of food and resources between the wealthy and poor nations would reduce the effects of many such disasters, but it would not eliminate them completely. Prior to this century, that is, before the development of effective means of communication and transportation (which themselves introduce different forms of suffering by way of collisions and consequent injuries and death) this alleviation of the effects of these natural evils was impossible; and even today it is not uncommonly impossible to do more than mitigate the extent of the evils.

There is also *the suffering caused by man to man and to animals.* Here it is necessary only to note what is going on in the war that is being waged at the time that this book is being read. (One does not need to be a cynic to believe that some war will be being waged somewhere in the world at most times.) Further, some on both sides will believe that what they are doing is morally right, even morally obligatory. In addition to this suffering, there is the evil which comes from unavoidable accidents consequent on human and animal behaviour. Many accidents, including motor accidents, are unavoidable, or avoidable only at the cost of accepting greater evils.

There is also *the vast misery,* fear, anxiety, grief, which *sincere, conscientious, and often godly men have caused.* Very often they have caused it because they blamelessly held and acted upon the basis of false beliefs. Consider here the pointless suffering caused by so many of the religious wars, by the Inquisition, and by personal, hurtful acts done for moral or religious reasons. In a world created by an omnipotent, omniscient, all-good God, one would expect to find no such evil, it arising as it does from a misdirected pursuit of the good. Immense suffering also results from the evil of *unavoidable error* of other kinds. (Some seek to explain all such erroneous belief and hence the suffering which comes from it as being due to sin, original sin, but this simply converts this problem into one that is even more perplexing.)

In addition to such suffering there is the suffering caused by *moral evil.* Moral evil, and the evil of the suffering that moral evil so commonly brings, are real evils. Moral evils are committed by most, possibly by all persons, at some time in their lives. Such evils arouse great indignation, most commonly when they are on the scale of the Turkish (as reported by Dostoevsky), Nazi, and those of recent years in Indo-China. Dostoevsky's report of the Turkish atrocities, because of its literary merits, conveys effectively the enormity of these evils and of the suffering they cause. Dostoevsky wrote:

" 'By the way, a Bulgarian I met lately in Moscow', Ivan went on . . . 'told me about the crimes committed by Turks in all parts of Bulgaria through fear of a general rising of the Slavs. They burn villages, murder, outrage women and children, and nail their prisoners by the ears to the fences, leave them till morning, and in the morning hang them – all sorts of things, you can't imagine. People talk sometimes of bestial cruelty, but that is a great injustice and insult to the beasts; a beast can never be so cruel as a man, so artistically cruel. The tiger only tears and gnaws and that's all he can do. He would never think of nailing people by the ears, even if he were able to do it. These Turks took a pleasure in torturing children too; cutting the unborn child from the mother's womb, and tossing babies up in the air and catching them on the points of their bayonets before their mother's eyes. Doing it before the mothers' eyes was what gave zest to the amusement. Here is another scene that I thought very interesting. Imagine a trembling mother with her baby in her arms, a circle of invading Turks around her. They've planned a diversion: they pet the baby to make it laugh. They succeed, the baby laughs. At that moment a Turk points a pistol four inches from the baby's face and blows out its brains. Artistic, wasn't it? By the way, Turks are particularly fond of sweet things, they say'." [1]

To date our concern has been with the causes of the evils of pain and suffering. It has been noted that much pain (where pain is treated as the felt, experienced, localized sensation as in a toothache) and suffering (felt as distress that is not localized in the body, e.g. as with fear, grief, anxiety) are caused by natural processes as in naturally caused privations, ageing, parasitivism, carnivorism, disease, natural disasters such as earthquakes, volcanoes, tidal waves, and the like.[2] However other causes, which are evils

---

[1] *The Brothers Karamazov,* London, Heinemann, 1945, trans. C. Garnett, p. 244.

[2] It is not being claimed here that this is the way in which pain and suffering are distinguished in ordinary usage, only that this usage notes an important, relevant distinction. Animals are often said to experience only localized pain, not suffering, and hence that the problem of physical evil as it relates to them is not serious. Neither claim is true. Animal pain presents a serious enough problem in itself; and animals may indeed suffer – consider the dog grieving over the loss of its master. It exhibits suffering, not pain behaviour.

Hick notes another relevant distinction thus:

"Whilst pleasure is a psychic condition, pain is a physical sensation with its own nerve structure. Pain in this sense has no opposite; it is simply a unique irreducible mode of sensation. On the other hand, the opposite of the psychic state of pleasure is the psychic state that is variously called unpleasure, suffering, discomfort, distress, anguish, negative hedonic tone, which I propose to call suffering." *Op. cit.,* p. 328.

Hick goes on to note that individuals may have pain sensations but not experience distress, i.e. pain awareness. Some, although apparently not Hick himself, who argue in this way seem to wish to suggest that animals may be like those who have pain

in themselves as well as for the suffering they cause have been noted, namely the evils of erroneous beliefs and of moral evil. More will now be
said in respect of the latter two evils.

That people should, in spite of all their efforts to the contrary, be committed to erroneous beliefs, especially moral and religious beliefs is itself
a grave evil. Clearly a world devoid of suffering and in which people were
doomed to live on the basis of erroneous beliefs would be a seriously imperfect world.

Moral evil requires much more lengthy treatment. Three types of moral
evil need to be distinguished. (a) Firstly there is that illustrated by the
person who is morally evil by way of neglecting to do what he ought to
do rather than by doing what is in itself intrinsically wrong. A man acts
in a morally evil way if he neglects to summon help for an accident victim
because he does not wish to be late for the start of a cricket match, he being
an opening batsman. His positive principle is morally innocent. His moral
fault lies in not adopting the appropriate principle. (b) Secondly, there is
the kind of evil illustrated by the evil person who acts on a principle which
he knows to be wrong. Thus the man who murders for gain, knowing that
murder is morally evil, is evil in this primary sense of morally evil. The
extreme kind of case here would be that of the person who acts for the
sake of evil, rather than for the sake of some good he sees. (c) A third,
puzzling kind of case is that of the person who sincerely believes to be the
true principles of morality, principles which in fact are false, evil principles.
Consider here the person who sincerely believes that it is not evil to be
cruel to animals *qua* being cruel to animals, or he who is a dutiful, conscientious racist, at the cost of an effort of will and suffering on his part (e.g.
a kind apartheidist). Where the moral error is not extreme we do not judge
such men to be morally evil. Where it is great, they are judged to be
extremely immoral men. What it is important to note here is that such
men are judged to be evil because they adopt and act on positively evil

---

sensations but not pain experience. Others seem to wish to argue from the fact that
pain sensations may as with soldiers and sportsmen under stress not result in awareness or experience of pain, that pain experience is preventable, or at least controll-
able by us. My impression, on the contrary, is that whilst we can cultivate the ability
to reduce the non-pain forms of suffering – e.g. those of envy, humiliation, fear,
anxiety – we have less ability to control the pain experiences which result from
pain stimuli. However in both areas individuals differ. In the case of suffering this
is partly due to the fact that developing some good character traits such as those
of concern for others, concern to do something worthwhile, exposes the persons concerned to forms of disappointment and distress and the like to which they would not
otherwise be exposed. To care deeply for others, and not to experience distress at
their misfortunes would be to be a worse person and a lesser person.

principles, and not because their actions simply lack the right principle. All who act on the basis of erroneous principles, including those who are praised as being morally virtuous, act in a way that causes their actions to lack the appropriate principle. All these accounts of moral evil, as moral evil, presuppose freedom of the will of some kind. Without freedom there can be no such evil as moral evil. This cannot be argued for at this stage, but will briefly be discussed in Chapter 8. It is sufficient here to note that this contention is basic to the celebrated solutions offered concerning the problem posed by moral evil.

Moral evil is seen by theists as being or involving a rejection of God. In so far as moral evil is seen as an evil which raises the question as to whether God exists, it needs to be construed in a more neutral way, as an intrinsic evil, whether or not God exists. Further, if it is to be seen as an evil of an ultimate character, distinct from the evil of physical evil (pain and suffering), it cannot be construed as it would be and is by most utilitarians. It might be argued by an utilitarian theist that there is only one ultimate problem of evil, that posed by physical evil. In agreement with those theists who acknowledge moral evil as an ultimate evil distinct from physical evil, I wish to stress that even if a solution could be found for the problem of physical evil, moral evil would still constitute a problem unless the solution to the former also encompasses the latter. There would in any case remain the problem posed by the evils of erroneous belief and of ugliness and aesthetic evil.

Ugliness and aesthetic evil. Aesthetic evils are real evils, and were the only evil in the world aesthetic evil, the theist would still be faced with the problem of reconciling the existence of such evil with the claim that the creator is all-powerful, all-wise, all-good. To create an ugly world or even an ugly object when the beautiful is possible is *prima facie* to manifest an imperfection. The imperfection is not a simple moral one, but it nonetheless relates to God's perfection as a wholly good being.

Many theists would seek to evade this problem by taking a subjectivist view of ugliness and aesthetic evil in general. It is not possible here to enter into the controversy concerning the objectivity or subjectivity of aesthetic excellence, but it is important to note that in so far as this manner of avoiding the problem of ugliness and aesthetic evil is adopted, to that extent the theist denies himself the right to praise God and his creations on aesthetic grounds where these involve an objectivist interpretation. Further, the subjectivist account of ugliness and of aesthetic evil would simply render such evils an aspect of physical evil, minor pains or suffering, and analogous with evils such as unpleasant tastes in foods which we are obliged to eat.

CHAPTER III

ETHICAL PRESUPPOSITIONS OF
THE PROBLEM OF EVIL

It has been traditional for theists and atheists to assume that the problem of evil is a real problem which may be stated on the basis of any meta-ethical theory at all, whether it be one which explains ethical judgments in terms of expressions of personal approvals, social attitudes, those of impartial observers, or one in terms of moral judgments as reports of objective facts about the world. Hick's insensitive, indeed, dogmatic discussion of good and evil, right and wrong, in *Evil and the God of Love,* whilst being a rather extreme example, is nonetheless a good illustration of this tendency. Hick writes:

"We have seen that from our human point of view, unaided by religious faith, that good is that which we welcome and the bad that which we would shun. The analogous theological definition will be in terms of the divine purpose for the created world. Whatever tends to promote the attainment of that purpose will be good and whatever tends to thwart it will be bad. The full and irreversible fulfilment of that plan would be the complete good sought by God in His activity in relation to His creation, whilst any final and irrevocable frustration of that plan would constitute irredeemable and ultimate badness.

The Christian concept of God's purpose for man enables the two kinds of evil – sin and suffering – to be bracketed together under their common contrariety to the divine purpose." [1]

Hick had suggested that the non-theological notion of bad, as distinct from wrong, springs from our having certain likes and dislikes, desires and aversions, and would not have developed otherwise, no argument being offered for this conclusion except an appeal to one line of philosophical thought, and this, in spite of the fact that there have been equally strong,

---

[1] Pp. 15 and 16. See also pp. 12, 13, e.g. "The basic reference of good, as a notion required by the human mind in its interaction with its environment, is to that which we like, welcome, desire, seek to gain, or to preserve, whilst bad refers to that which we dislike, fear, resist, shun and to which we are accordingly averse." p. 12.

opposed traditions of thought. Thus in the brief space of a few pages
Hick both reaches the conclusion that the bad thing is that which we dislike, do not welcome, etc., ignoring the fact that very often we like what
is bad and eschew that which is and is judged by us to be good, and also
uncritically defines or states, stipulatively but apparently unknowingly so,
the theological senses (i.e. the senses relevant to the problem of evil, *qua*
a problem) of good and evil. In the latter context he explains:

"The analogous theological definition will be in terms of the divine purpose for the created world. Whatever tends to promote the attainment of
that purpose will be good and whatever tends to thwart it will be bad." [2]

Later on in the book, when discussing the privation theory of evil, Hick
rejects the suggestion of J. S. Whale, myself and others, that the privation
theory, would if true, explain away the problem of evil, wholly it seems
on the basis of this early discussion, for no reason for this claim is offered
in the context of Hick's discussion of the privation theory.[3]

Hick's and similar accounts of bad and evil are to be rejected. When
the atheist and theist are formulating the problem of evil, they are not
formulating questions such as 'Does the Creator create things we dislike,
or do men perform actions other men dislike?'; 'Does the Creator of the
world realize his purposes in the world?' This is evident from the fact
that one of the doubts expressed by the question relates to whether God,
i.e. an all-perfect being, exists; another is that of questioning whether, if
there is a creator of the universe, he is all-perfect, and if not, whether he
and his purposes are good or partially or wholly evil. The traditional problem of evil is basically the set of problems set out in Chapter 1 concerning the existence of an all-perfect creator in the light of the fact of evil.
This is a problem which may be common to the believing theist, the agnostic, and the atheist. It is not a problem if Hick's account of the theological
senses of good and evil is accepted. Hick's problem is not a real one
for the person who denies the existence of God, or who has doubts about
it. For Hick the problem of evil becomes that of questioning the *competence* of an all-powerful creator in achieving his purposes. The question
of his goodness or badness in the light of evil becomes meaningless. God,
in terms of the theological senses of good and evil laid down by Hick, can
be neither good nor evil, only competent or incompetent; and, as will be
evident from later discussion in this Chapter, there is no real problem
of evil if evil is explained as it is by Hick in terms of his non-theological
sense. In any case there are well-known objections to attempts to explain

[2] *Ibid.*, p. 15.
[3] *Ibid.*, p. 187.

good and evil as they occur in the context of moral discussion and that of the problem of evil along the lines indicated by Hick. Students of ethics are familiar with the nature of these objections. More important, and more relevant to my immediate purpose, is my contention in this Chapter, that the problem of evil arises as the serious philosophical-theological problem it has traditionally been seen to be only on the basis of very different ethical presuppositions from those set out by Hick and many other theists. This can best be brought out by an examination of a number of accounts of good and evil, where the examination is designed to show how, if these accounts were true, there would be no problem of evil.

THE THEISTIC THEORY

An important theistic ethical theory is that according to which good is to be explained in terms of what God wills or approves, and evil as that which is contrary to the will or approval of God, where the goodness or evilness of things or actions exists only by virtue of God's approvals or disapprovals.[4] In terms of this account, the problem of evil could not consistently be formulated by the atheist. It is also difficult to see how it could arise as a perplexing problem for the theist who holds this ethical theory. How could there be a paradox or a suggestion of a contradiction in the facts that God is all-wise, all-powerful, unlimited, and the fact that there is evil such as pain and suffering in the world? From his power and wisdom we must conclude that God deliberately caused or permitted pain and suffering, and did so in his wisdom. If we could discover by independent means that God disapproves of the suffering in the world – and to do this is evidently impossible – the problem of evil would become that of exhibiting the rationality of God, of explaining his reason for freely creating that of which he disapproves. The point here is that this account of the nature of evil succeeds in disposing of the problem of evil by explaining God as a non-worshipful being, a supreme ruler, and not as a being who is good in the sense of good with which we normally operate. (He may or may not be such in terms of this latter sense.) There are some theists who are prepared to worship such an apparently unworshipful being – P. Geach adopts this course with no hint of apology or shame – but to do so is to worship power, not power and goodness and the associated perfections normally attributed to God.[5]

As an ethical theory, the theistic theory is evidently false. The relevant

---

[4] See for example "Religious Morality", by Patterson Brown, *Mind,* LXXII, 1963.
[5] *God and the Soul,* London, Routledge & Kegan Paul, 1969, esp. Chapter 9.

arguments have so frequently been set out in text books of ethics that they need not detain us long here. The basis of the most persistent objection is that we do not *mean* by good and evil what the theistic theory claims, and that this can be shown by reference to considerations including the above, and those pointed to before this century, and named in this century by G. E. Moore tests of "the naturalistic fallacy".[6] Thus we can meaningfully ask of that which is willed by the supreme creator, 'Is it good?'; we can commend what is so willed as being good without making a statement that has no force; and it is evident that no self-contradiction is involved in asserting that 'X is willed by an all-powerful, all-knowing being but it is not good'.

SUBJECTIVIST, NON-COGNITIVIST THEORIES

Good is often explained as being a word that is used to state or to express the speaker's likes, approvals, wishes, commands, prescriptions, preferences, pro-attitudes, and the like. If analyses along these lines were correct, none of the problems of evil indicated in Chapter 1 would arise. This is evident from the following considerations. If all we mean when we assert that pain, suffering, moral evil are evils, is that they evoke in us a con-attitude which we seek to express or to report by using the word evil, then there is no contradiction in the fact of their existence and the existence of the theist's God. The existence of phenomena in the world towards which we have a con-attitude is not a problem of the kinds noted in Chapter 1. There is no incompatibility between the existence of such objects and the claim that the Creator is an all-perfect being. It could be argued that a wholly good and benevolent God (i.e. a being towards whom we had pro-attitudes) would have created a world in which nothing existed towards which sentient beings would have con-attitudes (and that they would be such that none would have con-attitudes towards him), but such a problem, if it be a problem at all, is difficult to establish as a real problem. Certainly, it is very different from that of the traditional problem of evil. All of us have our likes and dislikes, for example, in respect of foods and smells; yet the existence of foods or smells we dislike is hardly a problem of the magnitude of the problem of evil, if it be a problem at all for the theist, and this in spite of the fact that pro- and con-attitudes towards foods and smells with many people matter more than do moral pro- and con-attitudes. However, as D. M. Armstrong has pointed out to me, there is a

[6] *Principia Ethica*, Cambridge, C.U.P., 1903, Chapter 1.

problem for the theist concerning consistency of attitudes, a problem relating to the rationality of a theism which involves disapproving of pain, suffering, moral evil, and yet approving of the cause of that which is disapproved of, God.

Further, if such an analysis, or some such kind of analysis is correct, another, different but equally serious problem would arise for the theist, namely that of explaining why a religious attitude of worship and adoration towards God should be adopted. To elaborate this point. If all we mean when we assert that God is good is that we have a pro-attitude towards him which we wish to have shared by others towards him, God comes to be defined simply as an omnipotent, omniscient, infinite being towards whom we have pro-attitudes. That is to say, he would not be the God who is worshipped as an all-perfect, wholly good being, for *he* lacks the one attribute, goodness, which is essential if he is to be deserving of worship, reverence, adoration, and obedience. His goodness becomes simply a purely contingent goodness, a response to him in us, and not an intrinsic attribute possessed by him. Different persons will have different attitudes. As already noted, there seems to be no rational basis for worship of power, even though there may be good prudential reasons for obeying the dictates of an all-powerful being. However the prudent course may often be a very immoral one. Thus the theist, in raising the problem of evil, is concerned with the goodness of God, where God's goodness is seen to be as much an attribute possessed by him as are his power, knowledge, wisdom and personal traits. This would seem to be essential if God is to be seen to be deserving of worship and not simply as a Geach-type God whom it is prudent to appear to worship, but perhaps immoral to obey.

OTHER ATTITUDE THEORIES

All attitude theories, whether they be relativist, Humean ideal observer theories, or attitude theories of other kinds, involve the same sorts of conclusions. They involve a redefining of the concept of God, so that the word "God" ceases to refer to a worshipful being. They thereby dissolve the apparent contradiction by showing that there is nothing to be explained by the theist. Consider relativism as the ethic which explains the good as that which is socially approved, where social approvals are backed by social sanctions, and the evil as that which is socially disapproved. (There are of course many versions of relativism.) How then is there any paradox in the claim that God, the socially approved, omnipotent, omniscient being, creates a world in which phenomena occur which are such as to arouse social disapproval, and in which men engage in acts which are disapproved of by the societies in which they live? Here it is to be noted that whether God is good or not – and this is distinct from being simply judged to be good – will depend on social attitudes towards him. His goodness therefore will be related to what are believed to be his works, and more basically still to human nature as shaped by its social environments. Thus if a society had pro-attitudes towards cruel and hurtful practices, members of that society would probably disapprove of a God believed to be a loving one, but approve of one who was a cause of pain and suffering.

Hume's ethic, according to which good is to be explained in terms of the feelings of the natural person, the impartial observer, involves the same sorts of implications.

THE PRIVATION ACCOUNT OF EVIL

Here it will be useful first to consider what is meant by those who seek to explain evil as a privation. St. Augustine, one of the major early proponents of the theory, explained it thus:

"For what is that which we call evil but the absence of good? In the bodies of animals, disease and wounds mean nothing but the absence of health; for when a cure is effected, that does not mean that the evils which were present – namely, the diseases and wounds – go away from the body and dwell elsewhere: they altogether cease to exist; for the wound or disease is not a substance, but a defect in the fleshly substance – the flesh itself being a substance and therefore something good, of which those evils – that is, privations of the good which we call health – are accidents. Just in the same way, what are called vices in the soul are nothing but privations of a natural good. And when they are cured, they are not transferred elsewhere: when they cease to exist in the healthy soul, they cannot exist anywhere else." [7]

Thus Augustine explained evil as being a lack, a loss, a privation.

Aquinas also advanced this privative theory of evil, for example, in *Summa Contra Gentiles*, Bk. 3, chapters 7 to 13, and in *Summa Theologiae* I, 48 and 49. In the former work Aquinas explained:

"Evil is simply a privation of something which a subject is entitled by its origin to possess and which it ought to have, as we have said. Such is the meaning of the word 'evil' among all men. Now, privation is not an

---

[7] *The Enchiridion, Basic Works of St. Augustine*, New York, Random House, 1948, trans. J. F. Shaw, ch. XI, p. 662.

essence; it is, rather, a negation in substance. Therefore evil is not an essence in things." [8]

Later on in the same work Aquinas, after noting again that evil is a certain privation, observed further:

"Besides, something is called evil due to the fact that it causes injury. But this is only so because it injures the good, for to injure the evil is a good thing, since the corruption of evil is good. . . . Thus, blindness injures a man to the extent that it is in him. So, evil must be in the good." [9]

In *Summa Theologiae,* after arguing thus:

"Every being, as being, is good. For all being, as being, has actuality and is in some way perfect; since every act implies some sort of perfection; and perfection implies desirability and goodness, as is clear from A. 1." [10]

Aquinas goes on to argue later:

"Evil imports the absence of good. But not every absence of good is evil. For absence of good can be taken in a privative and in a negative sense. Absence of good, taken negatively, is not an evil; otherwise it would follow that what does not exist is evil, and also that everything would be evil, through not having the good belonging to something else; for instance, a man would not be evil who had not the swiftness of the roe, or the strength of a lion. But the absence of good, taken in a privative sense, is an evil; as, for instance, the privation of sight is called blindness.

Now, the subject of privation and of form is one and the same – *viz.,* being in potentiality, whether it be being in absolute potentiality, as primary matter, which is the subject of the substantial form, and of privation of the opposite form; or whether it be being in relative potentiality, and absolute actuality, as in the case of a transparent body, which is the subject of both darkness and light." [11]

Gilson, commenting on Aquinas's writings, explained the theory in the following way:

"What is called an *evil* in the substance of a thing is only a lack of some quality which ought naturally to be there. For a man to have no wings is not an evil, because it is not the nature of the human body to possess wings. Similarly there is no evil in not having fair hair. The possession of fair hair is compatible with human nature but is not necessary to it. On the other hand it is an evil for a man to have no hands, while it is not so for a bird. Now the term *privation,* considered strictly and in its proper sense, desig-

---

[8] Chapter 7, sn. 2. Doubleday edition, translation by Vernon J. Bourke.
[9] *Ibid.,* Chapter 11, sn. 4.
[10] I, 5, 3.
[11] 1, 48, 3.

nates the absence or want of what a being ought naturally to possess. It is to privation of this kind that evil is limited. Evil is pure negation within a substance. It is not an essence, not a reality.

Since there is nothing positive about evil, its presence in the universe is unintelligible apart from the existence of real and positive subjects to support it. . . . Evil is not a being; all good, however, is being. . . . The mere absence of being cannot demand a subject to support it. But we have just said that evil is a negation in a subject, that is, a lack of what is normally a part of that subject; in a word, a privation. There can be no privation, and therefore no evil, without the existence of substances or subjects in which privation can be established. Thus it is not true that all negation demands a real and positive subject, but only those particular negations called privations, because privation is a negation in a subject. The only true support of evil is the good." [12]

And:

"Hence, finally, we can move on to a last conclusion, one which we must hold firmly, strange as it may seem; the cause of evil always resides in a good; and yet God, the cause of all good is not the cause of evil. From the foregoing considerations one thing remains clear: that whatever evil is reduced to a defect in some action, its cause is invariably a defect in the being which acts. Now there is no defect in God, but on the contrary a sovereign perfection. Evil, caused by a defect in the acting being, cannot be caused by God. But if we consider the evil which exists in the corruption of certain beings, we must on the contrary reduce it to God as its cause. . . . God therefore is the cause of corruptions and defects in all things but only because He wills to cause the good of the universal order, and, as it were, *per accidens* . . .

"Evil taken by itself is nothing. It is inconceivable that God can be its cause. If we ask what is its cause our answer is that it is the tendency of certain things to return toward non-being. . . . God has created them, it was because it was consonant with the divine perfection to form a more perfect image of Himself by expressing Himself in unequal creatures, some of which were corruptible, some incorruptible." [13]

C. Journet and J. Maritain, following Aquinas, stress the privative, or as it is otherwise characterised, the parasitic nature of evil. Journet, asking 'What is evil?', replies by offering as the definition, the following:

"Evil is a privation. But privation can be taken in two senses. Broadly

[12] E. Gilson, *The Christian Philosophy of St. Thomas Aquinas,* London, Gollancz, 1957, p. 156.
[13] *Ibid.,* p. 158.

speaking it can designate any lack or absence of good. In the strict sense privation is opposed to mere negation or absence; it is the *absence of some good which should be present*. This is the definition of evil." [14]

Journet then goes on to contrast this with the view that evil is something subsistent in its own right. Evil is, he contends, neither an illusion, nor a nothingness, nor a real existent, nor a substance. Hence he observes:

"To define evil as a privation is not to declare that it is non-existent and powerless. Privation moves away from nothingness in the same way as in mathematics do negative numbers from zero. It is inverted positivity, whose ravages can be limitless, and disastrous, in the order both of being and of action.

In the order of being, evil is not non-existent . . .

In the order of action, evil is not powerless. It can cause catastrophes . . .

Evil itself can corrupt good by being its *formal* cause . . . by taking the place of some form, quality or perfection which it destroys (blindness, dumbness, etc.)." [15]

And:

"The paradox of evil is the *terrible reality of its privative* existence." [16]

And:

"The importance of privation should be judged by the importance of what it destroys." [17]

Maritain's treatment of the nature of evil in *God and the Permission of Evil,* as Maritain acknowledges, draws heavily on Journet's account.

What is suggested by the foregoing extracts is confirmed by close reading of the sources from which they are taken, namely that no adequate explanations of the notions of "entitled", "proper", "ought", "should", "normal to", as used in the context of this theory are offered. All we find is the reference to a lack of an attribute, existence, or capacity natural, appropriate, or normal to the being. (What is appropriate is very different from what is natural, and both to what is normal to the being. All these various expressions will be found to occur in the extracts above.) Thus, in terms of this general view, baldness would be an evil, as would having eight instead of ten toes (even though no physical disability resulted), being born with two less teeth (but with wider ones), lack of an appendix, and the like would be privative evils in man, for in all these cases we lack organs appropriate to our species, that is, goods to which as members of the human

---

[14] *Op. cit.,* pp. 27-8.
[15] *Ibid.,* p. 48.
[16] *Ibid.,* p. 47.
[17] *Ibid.,* p. 48.

species we are "entitled", or which are such that they are "proper" to us, and which according to the order of nature we "ought" or "should" possess, where the "ought" or "should" is an ontological one, or again which are "natural" or "normal" to us as human beings. Thus, according to this theory, good equals being, and evil the privation of appropriate good or being; that is to say, evil is the absence of a good (being) which "ought" to be there. This "ought" is a metaphysical ought, and is explained as "proper to the being in terms of God's creative intention" in one of the statements of St. Augustine. This would suggest that evil, as privation, is more accurately to be explained as the absence of something that God planned should be there. If that is really the case, to explain evil as privation would be to restate the problem of evil as a problem relating to God's omnipotence or rationality, and not at all to his goodness. Clearly, proponents of the privation theory of evil do not intend this.

Evil as privation of proper good, and the reality of the problem of evil, if evil is so conceived. In "The Problem of Evil" I argued that if the privation theory of evil were true, there would be no problem of evil, that there would be no *prima facie* contradiction to explain. Everything God created would be good, and evil would be seen, not as a real presence or existence, or subsistence, but simply as a lack of a good usual, normal, natural, or proper to the species or act, as the case may be.[18] M. B. Ahern in "A Note on the Nature of Evil",[19] and J. Hick in *Evil and the God of Love*[20] reject this contention. Their reasons however are far from clear. With Hick it would seem to spring from his uncritical, dogmatic claim that one's view of the nature of evil is irrelevant to the question of the reality of the problem of evil. Argument against this contention has already been offered in this Chapter. Ahern's reasons for rejecting my contention may spring from confusing it with the significantly different although apparently similar view expressed by many, most recently by A. Flew, and which I should wish to reject as mistaken. Flew sets out his view that the privation theory seeks to explain evil as nothing thus:

"A more sophisticated move in the same area tries to exploit the thesis that all evil involves a falling short or a defect; hence it is ultimately essentially negative, and so, really nothing. This thesis is presented as the fruit of metaphysical analysis. It is, one fears, a prize example of the sort of thing which provoked the old saw: 'When a metaphysician says that this is really that, what he really means is that it is not, not really'. Whatever

[18] *Journal of Bible and Religion,* **XXX,** 1962.
[19] *Sophia,* **IV,** 1965.
[20] p. 187.

might be said for and against the thesis in some other context, it ought to be perfectly obvious that it can take no tricks here. If evil is really nothing then what is all the fuss about sin about: nothing? Nor would any attempt to depreciate as mere privations all those evils which in no way involve human choice easily escape the charge of subordinating compassion to ideological fancy. (See McCloskey, especially Sn. 2). This privation analysis was originally developed mainly in order to show, against Manicheism and Zoroastrianism, that evil is essentially a secondary and derivative principle. It has also been employed in hopes of showing that a Creator need not be – at any rate not *positively* and *directly* – the author of sin and other evils. The most sophisticated Thomists do not attempt to use it for the second somewhat different purpose (Copleston, pp. 143-150). On that operation Hobbes made in Chapter forty-six of *Leviathan* a curt, characteristic, decisive comment: 'This is vain philosophy. A man might as well say, that one man maketh both a straight line and a crooked, and another maketh their incongruity'." [21]

The contention that equating evil with privation amounts to equating it with nothing clearly needs more argument. There would seem to be an **obvious difference between nothing** and the absence of an appropriate good. None the less, Flew does here touch on an issue which worries some exponents of the theory, the very inappropriate talk about the power of evil, namely, the power of privations, of absences of being, and such like, in causing catastrophes, that is, other kinds of absences and privations. The talk about the power of evil is relevant to talk about evil, but not to talk about absences. Absences cannot exercise power.

As noted above, it might be argued from Augustine's account of evil as privation that this account does not dissolve the problem of evil, for privations amount to failures on God's part in realizing his intention. Those who press the privation theory do not wish to suggest this. They argue that God knowingly created a corruptible world knowing that things in it would be corrupted. God could have made a world of incorruptibles but did not. In making a world of corruptibles he knew what he was doing and intended to do what he did. There was no failure in God's power in his creating such a world, according to exponents of this theory. Where, then, is the problem of evil for them?

I suggest that for exponents of the theory there is no problem of evil, but only an illusion of a continuing problem due to "proper good", "entitled to be there", "naturally there", "ought to be there", being given a

---

[21] *Op. cit.*, p. 50.

moral interpretation which is incompatible with the theory. If good equals being, and privation, the absence of appropriate, natural being, there is no sense of evil according to which this absence of proper good can be said to be evil. The problem disappears. In fact, the writers concerned show that they hanker after another sense of evil according to which it is evil that an avoidable privation should occur. However, if evil is wholly explicable as privation, then it may well be asked 'What does it matter if beings capable of privations, develop or occur with privations?' It is possible, alternatively, that what lies behind the thought that the problem remains is not the unwitting use of another sense of evil, but simply the blind, unwarranted assumption expressed by Hick and others, that whatever be the meaning of the word evil, the problem of evil will remain a real problem. This is not so. The privation theory of evil renders the problem of evil not a real problem. Those theists who hold it are faced instead with two different problems. The one is that of showing why, if God is good only in the sense of good on which the theory operates, he merits worship. Mere being, even unlimited or pure being, whatever that may mean, is not a proper object of worship *qua* being. The other problem is that which may be posed by the question. 'Why did not God, if all-perfect, create a better world?' Even if it were true that this world is wholly good in the sense that everything in it is good, we can still properly ask why God did not do better by way of avoiding the kinds of privations he did not avoid. This is not the problem of evil so much as the problem of the less good world. More will be said concerning this problem later.

Thus, if true, the privation theory would imply that there is no problem of evil but other distinct problems, namely those of the worship-worthiness of the privationists' God, and of the justification of the less good, privative world. However, there are many grounds for questioning, indeed, rejecting this account of evil.

ASSESSING THE PRIVATION THEORY

A major objection to this theory relates to the account of good upon which it rests. The sense of good as being, as existence, is completely irrelevant to the sense in which the word good is used in formulating the problem of evil and has no direct relationship with our ordinary use of good, as for instance when we speak of pleasure, happiness, beauty as goods. What we are claiming when we say that pleasure is good, or that knowledge is good, is not that they are existents, but that they are the kinds of things it is desirable to seek to bring into existence because they possess value in themselves. We can and do talk meaningfully about non-existent goods which ought to be brought into being. So too, I suggest that the sense of evil that is relevant to our problem is distinct from any sense according to which evil is explained wholly in terms of privation of being. This may be brought out by the three considerations, namely, that it may be questioned whether all privations are evil, whether those privations which are evil are so *qua* privations, and thirdly, whether the obvious evils, pain, suffering, and moral evil admit of plausible explanation as privations. Before pursuing these questions one basic assumption of the privation theory needs to be examined.

The privation theory proceeds by reference to what is natural, proper, appropriate to the being, to what it ought to possess. Here there is an implicit reference to a belief in natural kinds, such that the being suffering a privation lacks an organ, attribute or capacity natural to members of his natural kind or class. In fact, as Locke and so many since have shown, this belief in the existence of sharply cut off natural kinds is open to challenge. This is confirmed by the evidence of evolutionary development. The evolving being lacks features possessed by that from which it has evolved but possesses new features. What meaning can be given to the notion of a privation in such cases? For instance, does the emu suffer a privation in lacking wings which would enable it to fly? In general we do not and ought not to regard a mutation as something suffering from privations, yet this theory would involve us in exactly this, where the mutation has not yet become an established new species. There is therefore an element of arbitrariness in what counts as a privation and it is no accident that Gilson in a passage above speaks of a privation as an absence of something which is *normally* present.

(i) If we disregard this general objection, we can go on to question the privation theory in the ways indicated above. Firstly we may ask whether all privations are evil. As the passages quoted earlier bring out, the exponents of the theory are very vague as to what count as privations. Examples which are indicated include as privations lack of organs, lack of attributes, and lack of capacities appropriate to the being. Lack of sight and lack of hands are cited as privations in man, lack of wings as not such. This leaves it unclear whether lack of hair on the head would be a privation in man. It is an existent feature or phenomenon in man, and as such the lack of it ought to count as a privation. So too with hair under the arms or on the legs. Yet it is hard to see that lack of hair under the arms or on the legs constitutes a privation which is an evil. On the contrary, in women such a privation may be valued as an excellence. Similarly, it is arguable that baldness is thought to be an evil in our society only because of our aesthetic or social preferences, and even so, with the development of synthetic wigs, this seems to be becoming less true. A society could well prize baldness as aesthetically pleasing, and as an excellence, and come to regard hairiness as we now regard facial hairs in women. So too, lack of two toes is a lack of a proper good, namely two organs naturally possessed by human beings. Yet if the remaining eight toes were large and performed the function of toes well, it would be implausible for the person suffering the privation to claim to be suffering a real evil. None the less if, because of the beliefs of his society that eight-toed men were inferior and discriminated against as such, the man suffered humiliations and hurts, then we might accept his claim that his lack of toes was an evil. This would be to make what counts as a privation and an evil culturally relative, and dependent on social and/or cultural beliefs. Any human traits, including most human excellences, admit of being viewed unfavourably by society, and the person possessing the excellence can come to be exposed to hurt as a result. This occurs in sub-groups in respect of height, high intelligence, male and female beauty, and the like. Yet this does not render the excellence any less an excellence. The same should hold of what are privations and evils.

Consider also useless organs, for example, the appendix. A person born without an appendix lacks an organ but not a capacity in the usual sense of capacity. He cannot because of his lack of this organ claim that he is suffering a privation which is an evil. This example may suggest that the concept of a privation should be explained in terms of a lack of a capacity or capacities rather than in terms of lack of proper organs. This however would seem not to be a permissible move. Capacities spring from the possession of organs, such that where there is a defective capacity or lack of a capacity, we find either a mal-functioning in the organ (due to some other privation) or the absence of the relevant organ. Yet the evil complained of is the lack of the capacity in many cases. In other cases, as with baldness, the privation involves no lack of a capacity. Further, in other contexts we accept that a being may lack a capacity natural to a species and yet not be suffering from a privation which is an evil. It is a capacity of human beings that they can do most things better with their right hands than with their left hands. (The lack of this ability is parallel with deafness or blindness or colour-blindness in certain respects – the left-handed person cannot do things which it is important that he be able to do in our society, but he can do other things the right-handed man cannot do. So too the deaf and the blind develop capacities the non-deaf and the sighted do not have.) The lack of this normal human excellence, that is, this kind of privation is no evil if it is compensated for by unusual ability in the use of the left hand, and if there are no social penalties for being left-handed. Other privations may be valued as boons, and not as evils. This could be the case with lefthandedness, as in a boxer, or as with sterility occurring in a mother of many children and who would be killed by another pregnancy. This again suggests both that there are difficulties in seeking to explain privations in terms of lack of capacities, and all lacks of natural capacities as evils.

There are privations of organs that we regard as evils, even where the remaining organ performs the function of two organs well, for example, where the one kidney of the person born lacking a second kidney performs the function of the two completely satisfactorily. This is simply because we believe the possessor of the one kidney to be more vulnerable to injury and disease than is a person with two kidneys. If a one-kidneyed man lived a full life and died at the age of ninety without ever suffering ill-effects from his possessing only the one kidney, it would be absurd to argue that because he suffered the privation of a major organ, he suffered from an evil all his life. Consider here the case of such a man about whom it is discovered only in a post-mortem examination, that he lacked a kidney. There are difficulties therefore in explaining privations which are evils solely in terms of lack of organs.

Privations commonly cited by the exponents of the theory are blindness, deafness, dumbness. The evils complained of here are not the lack of or defects in the relevant organs but the lack of a valued capacity or capacities. The blind man complains that he cannot see, not that he has a defective eye. If by a miracle he could be made to see even with the eye remaining defective, he would no longer complain of his privation. Yet it may be argued here that it is not so much the lack of a capacity which is seen to be evil but rather the fact that lack of the capacity deprives the individual from access to goods, and exposes him to evils. The blind man cannot experience the pleasures of sight, and is exposed to risk of injury and starvation because he is ill-equipped to care for himself.

Death is probably unique in being a privation which is regarded as being evil *qua* privation. Death, the ceasing to exist, seems to most people to be an evil, yet it is essentially a privation. I suggest that it is seen as an evil because it usually involves the loss of goods which have been enjoyed and valued. The person who takes his own life does not necessarily see death as an evil, a lesser evil. He may see it as a valued termination of an evil state of consciousness or of existence and thereby see the privation as a good.

(ii) It is now necessary to consider whether that which is evil, is always a privation, and evil *qua* being a privation. Pain, suffering, moral evil, and lack of certain necessary, useful excellences are the main evils which will be considered here. If we turn to the writings of exponents of this theory we again find them to be less illuminating and of less help than might reasonably have been expected. Pain and suffering are two of the great evils, with which the problem of evil is concerned, yet, as Gilson's exposition of Aquinas's discussion (*Summa Theologiae*, I, II, 35) brings out there is no real facing up to the problem of showing that the evilness of pain and suffering consists in their being privations. Gilson here writes:

"The opposite of pleasure is pain. Taken as a passion in the strict sense, pain is the sensitive appetite's perception of the presence of evil. This evil affects the body, but it is the soul that suffers. Corresponding to joy, a mental apprehension of good, we have here grief, caused by an internal apprehension of some evil. Grief does not imply the complete absence of joy. We can, for example, be sad about one thing and joyful about something else unrelated to it. Grief and joy are also perfectly compatible when their objects are contraries. Thus to rejoice about the good and to grieve over evil are two closely related sentiments. Moreover, there is a joy that has no contrary grief; the joy of contemplation, for example, has no contrary. When contraries are grasped by the intellect, they contribute to the knowledge of truth. Moreover, since intellectual contemplation is the work of thought, fatigue and weariness have no part in it. Only indirectly that is, through the exhaustion of the sense faculties which the intellect uses, do weariness and sadness keep man from contemplating.

Pain and grief are caused by the presence of evil and result in a general diminution of activities in the one who experiences them . . . Grief can affect physiological as well as psychological activity." [22]

The suggestion here is not that pain and suffering are evils, and evils *qua* being privations, but rather that they are in a sense goods which are responses to privations, in the case of pain to privations in the body. There is also a suggestion, made explicitly by Journet that they are evils or have an evil aspect in so far as they take away the peaceful enjoyment of a good which ought to be there. Journet here observes:

"1. Is not pain, though, the cruellest and most tyrannical of realities? It is the awareness, by means of our ability to feel of an irregularity or privation; the tactile perception, sometimes useful as a warning, sometimes merely registering it, of any alteration to an organ. It can be broken down

---

[22] *Op. cit.*, pp. 282-3.

into two elements: a positive one, namely knowledge, and a privative one, namely disordered biological activity." [23]

"Given the presence of some evil, says St. Thomas, it is good that sadness or pain should result: their absence would mean that the evil has not been felt or recognized for what it is.

Hence pain and suffering are not ranked in the first place among forms of evil because they are identical with knowledge and awareness, but only because they are knowledge and awareness of a disorder or privation.

2. Pain and sorrow themselves, however, are an evil, but only inasmuch as they take away the peaceful enjoyment of a good which ought to be there. All the same the evil of sorrow may, on a higher plane, turn into good; and sorrow itself may become good, for example, when it arises from the evil of sin being recognized as such by a righteous mind and detested as such by a righteous heart." [24]

Pain: Clearly this will not do. Pain is an evil over and above the evil which causes it. The headache, the toothache, the pain that comes with broken ribs, are distinct evils from the evils of a temperature, a decayed tooth, of broken bones. Further, the pain need not be proportional to the bodily disorder. A slightly decayed tooth may pain a lot, a very badly decayed one not at all. The pain may not be related to an organic cause – consider the sympathetic pain experienced by the husband whose wife is in labour. It is felt pain that we rightly complain of as an evil. It is the pain of the toothache that we wish to be rid of – that is why, if the pain ceases many persons choose not to have the diseased tooth attended to.

Further, if we construe the pain that requires explanation as a privation as the felt sensation, and one which results from the sensation through the nerves, then the experience of feeling pain is as real and as positive an experience as that of the experience of colour which results from observing a coloured object; and the felt pain can no more be explained as a privation, a lack, an absence of something, than can the experience of yellow when observing a yellow object.

Perhaps, as others have suggested, it will be argued that pain is not itself a privation, but that its evilness consists in its involving a privation. Its evilness, it might be claimed, consists in pain depriving us of a state of contentment. This is how Journet argues. I suggest that such a move is a desperate one, and as implausible as attempts to explain a colour, for

[23] *Op. cit.*, p. 36.
[24] *Ibid.*, pp. 36-7. See also M. B. Ahern's "A Note on the Nature of Evil", *Sophia*, IV, 1965, and also his discussion in *The Problem of Evil*, pp. 18-19.

example green, as consisting in the absence of red, yellow, blue, orange, etc.

Suffering: Suffering may have no connection at all with ill-health in the organic body, and may, indeed often does, spring from health in the mind as for example with grief at misfortune overtaking a loved one, or as with anxiety in a mother when her child is gravely ill. The evil, suffering, is a positive thing. The suffering that comes from grief, despair, humiliation, anxiety, is as real as the pleasures and contentment of friendship, aesthetic appreciation, love, success in one's endeavours; it is as positive a phenomenon, and to seek to explain the former in terms of the latter, is to misunderstand and misrepresent the nature of the former. Further, as with pleasure and happiness, I suggest that we see the evilness of suffering to be a consequential property. It is by virtue of the natures of pleasure and happiness that they are good; it is the nature of suffering that renders it evil. If asked 'Wherein consists the evil of pain or of suffering?' we should be at a loss for an answer in the same way as we should be if asked 'Wherein consists the goodness of pleasure?' With intrinsic goods we can simply point to the character of the good, as pleasure, happiness, rationality, etc. So too with intrinsic evils. There too we can simply point to the character of that which is deemed to be intrinsically evil.[25]

Moral Evil: Moral evil is also explained by exponents of the privation theory as consisting in a privation. In the *Summa Theologiae,* St. Thomas Aquinas, in answer to the question, "Whether Vice is contrary to Nature?", replied:

"*I answer that,* As stated above (A. 1), vice is contrary to virtue. Now the virtue of a thing consists in its being well disposed in a manner befitting its nature, as stated above (A. 1). Hence the vice of any thing consists in its being disposed in a manner not befitting its nature, and for this reason is that thing vituperated, which word is derived from *vice* according to Augustine. (D Lib. Arb. iii, 14).

But it must be observed that the nature of a thing is chiefly the form from which that thing derives its species. Now man derives his species from his rational soul: and consequently whatever is contrary to the order of reason is, properly speaking, contrary to the nature of man, as man; while whatever is in accord with reason, is in accord with the nature of man, as man. Now man's good is to be in accord with reason, and his evil is to be against reason, as Dionysius states (Div. Nom. iv). Therefore human virtue, which makes a man good, and his work good, is in accord with

---

[25] See G. E. Moore, *Principia Ethica,* pp. 209-214.

man's nature, for as much as it accords with his reason: while vice is contrary to the order of reason." [26]

H. Meyer explains Aquinas's view of moral good and evil thus:

"The order of values and ends is proposed to the will by the intellect. Now the statement, the good depends on the object and on the right end, is developed to mean that moral goodness of the will depends on the conformity to the order of reason. Aquinas goes farther in the development of this idea when he says that in a higher degree morality depends on conformity with the eternal law, and ultimately with God. By his very nature man carries within himself the seal of the divine intelligence in the form of the general principles of action according to which the ends and purposes of his strivings are measured. The proximate rule for the acts of the will is the human reason; the supreme rule is the eternal law and the will of God that it gives expression to. The moral act derives its quality from its agreement or non-agreement with some norm. This norm and rule is derived ultimately from God and is expressed in the *lex aeterna*. Human reason is able to comprehend this norm; indeed much of the order of value and worth is revealed in natural happenings which are governed by divine law. The moral phenomenon is only part of the universal world phenomenon." [27]

And:

"Evil or sin is a defection from the order of reason, which is the same as the divine order of the universe; it is an act of the free will which robs man of his dignity and degrades him to an animal servitude." [28]

I suggest that this attempt to explain moral evil as a privation is no more successful than are the attempts to explain pain and suffering as privations. It involves both an oversimplification and distortion of the facts. As noted earlier, the extreme type of morally evil action is more accurately described, and its evilness explained, in terms of there being an evil principle deliberately adopted in the knowledge that it is wrong. The sort of case that is relevant here is that of the person who knows that the killing of innocent persons is wrong, but who none the less makes it his principle of action, the principle of killing for gain whenever it is safe to do so. Another kind of morally evil action noted earlier is that which involves adopting a morally neutral principle of action in a situation in which a moral principle was relevant, for example, ignoring the needs of another when

[26] I, II, 71, 2.

[27] *The Philosophy of St. Thomas Aquinas,* St. Louis, Herder Book Co., 1944, trans. E. Eckhoff, pp. 377-8.

[28] *Ibid.,* p. 383.

one is engaged in the otherwise morally harmless pursuit of one's pleasure – for example continuing with one's fishing when a child nearby is drowning and whom one could easily save. Here we have a morally evil action, and the evilness springs from a failure to act on the basis of the relevant rule. Yet even here we should more properly explain the evilness of the act in terms of the implicit adoption of a positive rule, namely that of pursuing one's own pleasure without regard for the well-being of others. In each case I suggest that the evil of the morally evil act results from the presence and adoption of the wrong rule and that the evil act is a reality, a positive thing, and not simply an act which lacks conformity with the rule of reason. It results from a positive presence, and the evilness is a real feature of the action that is morally evil.

Can evil be self-subsistent? Can good be self-subsistent? A major point made by exponents of the privation theory is that evil is parasitic on good (being, existence), and cannot be self-subsistent. Evil cannot exist in isolation. This is rightly said to be true of evils such as pain, suffering, disease. For there to be pain there must be a being who is experiencing the pain; so too with disease and suffering. More basically, one cannot have pure evil; evil is always a feature of something existent in some way. However, these truths are irrelevant to the truth or falsity of the privation theory. One can no more have pure health, pleasure, happiness, contentment, than pure pain, suffering, or disease. There must be an organism or being which is healthy, experiencing pleasure, happiness, contentment. Further, one can no more have pure goodness, good existing alone, than one can have evil existing alone. What one finds are good things, good men, good actions; as with evil, evil things, evil men, evil actions, evil states of affairs. This does not imply that good and evil are not real phenomena. We think of colours, hardness, and other properties of physical objects as real features of things, yet they cannot be self-subsistent. So, too, with the lack of self-subsistence of good and evil. It is noteworthy that the two outstanding exponents of ethical objectivism in this century, G. E. Moore and W. D. Ross relate their defence of their theories to "good" being the name of a supervenient or consequential property.[29] That the theist is committed to the reality of good, and, in the context of the acknowledgement of the problem of evil as a real problem, to the reality of evil, is evident from the insistence on God as an object of worship in the full sense of worship. Mere power, no matter how great, is not a proper or fitting object of worship. Some positive reference to goodness as real is required to ren-

[29] See G. E. Moore, *Principia Ethica*, Chapter 1 and W. D. Ross, *The Right and the Good*, Oxford, Clarendon, 1930, pp. 121-4.

der the concept of God a genuinely religious concept. And, as argued in this Chapter, unless evil is real, there is not even an apparent contradiction between God's goodness as an all-powerful creator, and the evil in this world.

A final point concerning the privation theory might be noted here. Exponents of the theory attribute causal power to evil and to evil beings, and it is true that we do think of evils and of evil things as being capable of becoming causes. Pain and suffering may cause persons to act in various ways – consider here the use of torture. And morally evil persons, and evil spirits (if they existed) could be causes. Consider here the Hitlers, the Stalins, the Eichmanns; consider too the way some theists seek to explain the existence of evils such as calamities, suffering, and even moral evil in men, as a result of the activities of evil spirits, where the evil spirits are thought of as causes of these results. However the whole notion of evil as a cause, or as a causal force, fails on the privation theory. An absence of a proper X, an X which ought to be there, cannot be a cause.

It is true that we do in everyday talk about causes speak of absences as causes. For example, we speak of the absence of food, starvation, as the cause of the starved individual's death; we speak of the lack of oxygen as the cause of the death of the person who dies as a result of a faulty gas heater; and so on. However, this is an inaccurate, shorthand mode of speech. The cause of death through starvation would positively be spelt out in terms of the chemical or bio-chemical changes in the body of the person, i.e. positively. In the case of death due to lack of oxygen, the true cause might well be explained in terms of carbon-monoxide and the effects of carbon-monoxide on the human organism. All this relates to a more general feature of day to day talk about causes. Just as we so often select one factor or condition out of hundreds of equally important factors – because we wish to stress it perhaps as one we can or ought to control, so too with absences referred to as causes. Consider the explanations that can be given concerning the cause of an accident. The accident occurred because the driver was drunk, because he drove too fast, because the road was slippery, because the other driver was inexperienced and dithered instead of acting swiftly and decisively, etc. So too, when we single out a lack or an absence as a cause, as in the latter explanation. By preventing the lack of food occurring, that is by providing food, or by lowering the carbon-monoxide level or eliminating its cause, the undesired event can best be prevented. This however simply shows that there is a lack of precision and completeness in ordinary talk about causes. When tightened up, no one single factor can be said to be *the* cause. Equally, no absence or lack can feature as an integral, essential part of a complete causal explanation. Positive presences are what enter into carefully stated scientific causal explanations. This fact means that an important, positive element is absent from the privative analysis of evil. It cannot adequately explain the roles of evils as causes.

EVIL AS UNREAL

Three other avenues are open to those who seek to deny the reality of the problem of evil. It may be argued that the concept of evil is a pseudo- and not a real concept, and hence that evil is an illusion. Alternatively, it may be argued that there are no real evils, that all apparent evils *are* merely apparent evils. Or thirdly it may be argued that all evil phenomena are mere appearances and not realities. The foregoing discussion bears on the first of these lines of argument, that evil is not a real but only a pseudo-concept. There is no internal incoherence in the concept of evil. The discussion of the privation theory bears on the second line of argument; if the contentions there are sound this contention too must be rejected. However the privation theory is not the most extreme version of the claim that evils are not real evils if properly understood. There is another traditional, persistent line of argument to this same end, one which occurs in purported solutions to the problem of evil to the effect that evil is like a discordant or ugly element in a symphony or painting but one which in fact adds beauty to the whole work. Although this is not normally treated as the contention that evil is unreal, it amounts to no less than this. The discord is not a real discord, the ugliness is not really ugliness, the evil is not really evil, in each case the whole or the complex is enriched, made better by the apparent evil. It is important that it be noted here that this argument from analogy by reference to the arts does not seek to justify evil as a means to good; it is an argument that the so-called evils are essential components or ingredients of goods, and hence not real evils.

There are obvious difficulties in the way of such an account, the most obvious one being that it implies that we should be cautious about eliminating evils. Indeed if all evil is of this kind we should never eliminate evil, for it is, when properly understood, seen really to be good. This leads on to a morally abhorrent thesis about which more will be said in Chapter 8.

In respect of the third kind of claim, that all apparent evils are not really real, and hence that there are no real evils in existence, the discussion of the facts which give rise to various of the problems of evil, particularly Problems 2 and 3 as stated in Chapter 1, is an adequate reply. None the less, thoughtful theists have sought to deal with the problem of evil in these various ways. Mary Baker Eddy, and those of the Christian Science faith, appear to adopt the third course, of suggesting that false belief is involved in accepting the reality of evils such as pain, disease, suffering and death. Mrs. Eddy wrote, for example:

"The Christian Scientist has enlisted to lessen evil, disease, and death; and he will overcome them by understanding their nothingness and the allness of God, or good. Sickness to him is no less a temptation than is sin, and he heals them both by understanding God's power over them. The Christian Scientist knows that they are errors of belief, which Truth can and will destroy." [30]

This and other passages in which the nothingness of evil is alluded to suggests that on this view, all evils, properly understood, are seen to be "nothing". Yet the talk about God's power over evils, and that evils are a temptation, suggest a more positive view along the lines of a parallel with the false belief that a mirage is a real lake. It might be said that a mirage too is a nothingness. In fact, it is a real mirage, but not a real lake. In the case of pain and suffering, such an analogy breaks down − "false" belief that one is in pain or that one is suffering, involves real pain and suffering, i.e. false belief that one is in pain or that one is suffering is impossible, although it is possible to be mistaken about the location of the pain, or the cause thereof, and about the kind of suffering. So too, given the dictionary definition of disease as: "Morbid condition of body, plant, or some part of them, illness, sickness; any particular kind of this with special symptoms and name; ... " (*Concise Oxford Dictionary*), there can be no question that disease occurs. Mrs. Eddy makes reference to dreams and to their unreality becoming evident when they are seen to be dreams. Yet a dream is real as a dream; and moral evil, suffering and pain, when seen for what they really are, and not simply as they might appear to be, are seen to be full realities.

CONCLUSION

The object of this Chapter has been to show that good and evil must be attributed objective reality of some kind if the problem of evil is to arise as a serious problem for the theist. Difficulties in the way of attempts to deny the objective goodness of a worshipworthy God, and the objective reality of evils such as pain, suffering, and moral evil have also been noted.

[30] *Science and Health with Key to the Scriptures,* (Authorised edition) p. 450.

CHAPTER IV

THE NATURE AND ATTRIBUTES OF GOD

Besides the ethical presuppositions of the problem of evil, there is the presupposition that God is a being who literally possesses the attributes of omnipotence, omniscience and goodness. Various proposed solutions seem to presuppose that other attributes, such as being a person or having personal traits, including that of loving his human creations, also hold of God in a literal sense and not in some non-literal, symbolic, metaphorical, or some other sense. It is therefore important to consider whether the problem of evil does presuppose the literal ascription of the former attributes to God, and if so, what in particular is involved in a literal ascription of the attributes of omnipotence, omniscience and goodness, and whether the solutions which refer to God's personal and loving nature can consistently interpret these traits literally.

This inquiry is important because very many theists who accept the problem of evil as being a real one, when they discuss and analyse the attributes of God outside the context of the problem of evil, have been reluctant to explain them in a literal sense. This being so, it is necessary to consider the senses in which the attributes of God are predicated with a view to seeing whether the problem of evil remains a real problem for such theists, and if so, how and in what ways. It will be argued that the non-literal ascription of attributes to God, involves the theists concerned in a committal to a view of God as a finite and limited being, and that whilst they may thereby escape the problem of evil, this is not a necessary consequence of this kind of account of the attributes of God, for the problem of evil may arise in the forms set out in Chapter 1 as Problems 4 and 5. Further, there will arise the additional problem of explaining the worship-worthiness of the God so-explained.

Here the views to be examined range from the literalist view, that God is literally omnipotent, omniscient and all-good, through that of Mansel and others that God's attributes are unknowable, to the contemporary views that the attributes of God are knowable but do not admit of literal expression or communication.

GOD'S ATTRIBUTES AS LITERALLY ASCRIBED

A great variety of attributes are ascribed to God. Some are purely negative for example, the attributes of being intangible, invisible, and the like. Others are the so-called pure perfections, life, power, intelligence, wisdom, goodness. Others again are of a kind which, if literally interpreted, would involve limitations, for example, being a person, a father, one who loves his creations, and the like. My contention here is that for the problem of evil to arise in its traditional form for the theist, the attributes of power, wisdom and knowledge, as well as goodness must hold of God in a literal sense. Since apologists who accept the problem as a real one often seek to advance solutions by reference to other alleged attributes of God, attributes such as that he is a personal God who loves mankind, and who is capable of personal relationships with his creations, it will be useful here to consider these attributes, and how and in what sense God could be understood to possess them, as well as the more primary attributes of omnipotence, omniscience, and goodness.

Omnipotence. On the face of it the literal ascription of unlimited power to God presents few difficulties. We understand by power the ability to sustain or to bring about a change, an existence, or the destruction of a thing or a state of affairs; a being has power in that it has the ability to do or to refrain from doing something; we have power in so far as we have the ability to do or refrain from doing various things. Omnipotence is often explained as the power to do anything and everything that is possible. As G. H. Joyce notes:

"Even those who affirm the absolute infinity of God's power, admit that there are things which He cannot do: e.g. that He cannot bring it about that two plus two make five, or that the past should not have happened." [1]

And:

"Infinite power can realize all things. The objects excluded from omnipotence are so because they are not things at all, but no-things, and hence incapable of realization by reason of their nonentity, not by reason of lack of power in God. It may be well to illustrate each of these two sources of impossibility. Notions which contain contradictory elements are not being. ... Again, it is no diminution of omnipotence that God cannot do those things which are inconsistent with infinite perfection, and only possible to a finite agent." [2]

[1] *Op. cit.*, p. 415.
[2] *Ibid.*, pp. 416-7.

As these statements bring out, in ascribing power – unlimited power or omnipotence to God – the theist is not involved in understanding "power" in some sense other than that in which we speak of the power a man possesses. Omnipotence, or all-power, is power greater than all other beings possess and such as not to be limited in any way by the power of lesser beings whose power is dependent on that of the omnipotent being. An omnipotent being can do anything that is possible. It cannot do what is logically impossible for the logically impossible is not something – as Joyce brings out, the logically impossible is a non-thing. An omnipotent being is often spoken of as an infinitely powerful being. This, I suggest, is to introduce a needlessly obscure notion, that of infinitely, into the account. It is presumably a way of saying that there are an infinite number of possible things that may be done, infinite possibilities for the exercise of power, and that an all-powerful being can do all that is possible. This, I suggest, is unhelpful, as the notion of possibility here is logically subordinate to the notion of unlimited power; the possibilities are all those things an all-powerful being can do. In the light of these considerations, it is surprising that any theist should wish to ascribe power, all-power or omnipotence, to God in any but a literal sense. The sense in which God has power, is that in which we are ascribed power. God's power is simply greater and such as to make our power not simply subordinate to but dependent on his power.

It is possibly because of the paradoxes that arise in respect of God's omnipotence that some theists have sought to explain omnipotence in a non-literal way. Most of the paradoxes turn on a confusion between what an all-powerful being may do and must do, or on incompatibilities between omnipotence and other divine perfections. Thus it is suggested that there is a paradox springing from whether the omnipotent being can destroy itself, or whether it can make something indestructible or immovable – instantaneously or over a period of time – or the like. I suggest that these are not real paradoxes, that either a logical impossibility is being indicated (e.g. with instantaneous self-destruction, creation of an indestructible body), or that God can do what is described, but if he did he would become a being which was no longer omnipotent.

The paradoxes arising from God's omnipotence and his other perfections are more serious. Joyce here observes:

"Yet God's inability to do evil places no restriction on Him or His omnipotence." [3]

---

[3] *Op. cit.*, p. 420.

I suggest that Joyce is mistaken in respect of omnipotence here. Clearly, an omnipotent being must be able to do what is evil unless by the nature of the case it is logically impossible for it to do so. The question of the possibility of an omnipotent being, being able to change moral and value standards is more puzzling. Many would wish to argue that to do so is logically impossible. My own view is that a synthetic *a priori* impossibility is involved, and hence that it is impossible for a being to be omnipotent in the sense indicated above. Whether the impossibility is a synthetic *a priori* one or not raises many issues that cannot be pursued here. The important issue is that if there are impossibilities of this kind they involve limitations other than those due to logical impossibilities on God. One must either reject God's omnipotence or the fact of synthetic necessary connexions and impossibilities. Many theists are committed to the fact of the latter, whilst seeking to insist on God's omnipotence, in their proofs of the existence of an all-perfect, omnipotent God.

It has also been argued that it is mistaken to argue that God can, by virtue of his omnipotence, do anything at all, for example, something silly. Could an all-powerful being cause a sign to appear in the sky saying 'Fortitude beer is best' simply as a result of a whim? I suggest it must be able to do so. That we do not think that God would do so is because we attribute to him other perfections besides omnipotence. This relates to a more general issue which will be discussed later in this Chapter concerning whether the various perfections attributed to God are logically compatible with one another.

Omniscience. The concept of omniscience is also one which presents no difficulty in respect of its literal interpretation, but again, it is one which leads to apparent or actual paradoxes. To be all-knowing means exactly that, namely to know all that has been, all that is, and all that will be, all that can be. Omniscience is implied in omnipotence, for a being which lacked knowledge would lack the power to achieve what it wished to achieve.

The paradoxes which arise from omniscience chiefly relate to the conjunction of omniscience and other perfections of God, most notably, omnipotence and goodness, and to alleged perfections in man, for example, freedom of the will.

Goodness. Another attribute of God is goodness. God is said to be wholly good in the sense of being wholly morally perfect, willing always what is good, as well as being perfect in all other respects. I suggest that there is no difficulty in understanding the notion of perfect goodness, and that there is no need, nor indeed possibility of understanding this goodness in a sense other than that which applies to human beings. God is wholly good in the sense in which moral agents in general, according to their natures and contexts and powers, strive to be good.

The paradox which arises in respect of God's goodness relates to the question as to whether God is contingently or necessarily good. A being who is contingently good but who may conceivably be evil, may be wholly good in one sense, but lack perfection in another. A being who could not be evil, who is not contingently good but such that we can be certain it will always be good, would appear to be superior in goodness. This is how orthodox Christians see the goodness of God. For them, God cannot commit evil. They explain this in terms of there being no possible motives or reasons for evil for God. The problem or paradox that arises here relates to whether God is thereby necessitated to good, and if so, whether the necessitation to goodness is real goodness. A human person necessitated to act virtuously would typically not be deemed to be virtuous (unless one accepts the compatibility thesis, that free will and determinism are not incompatible, a thesis which is commonly founded on the much questioned paradigm case argument, and which I should wish to reject for this and for independent reasons which cannot be gone into here); yet an omnipotent being who *might* be evil, indeed who could be evil, seems less than perfectly good.

The Compatibility of the Perfections of God. This issue, as it arises in this context, is that of the compatibility of complete power, knowledge, wisdom and goodness. Omnipotence involves the power to do anything that is logically possible; perfect goodness involves the impossibility in some sense of doing what is evil. If moral principles are synthetic necessary truths, they impose a limitation on the power of all beings which is a limitation other than that due to logical impossibility. Wisdom imposes a limitation in that a perfect being *cannot do* silly things, by virtue of his perfection, wisdom. Omniscience involves further difficulties in respect of omnipotence and goodness. A being cannot be omnipotent in the sense of achieving what it seeks to achieve without wisdom and knowledge. Yet if the omnipotent being is necessarily omniscient the problem arises as to how an omnipotent being can be wholly good and yet create, with foreknowledge and without pre-determination, beings who will be morally evil.

It would seem to be the more useful course at this stage to leave these issues, and to look now at how theists, when they are not explicitly concerned with the problem of evil, seek to explain these attributes of God. My thesis here is that much contemporary theistic theory, and even traditional theology, seek to explain the attributes of God in a way which avoids the traditional problems of evil, noted as Problem 1 and 2 in Chapter 1, and instead explain God's attributes in terms of him being finite or limited in some respect or respects. This may be brought out by considering a sample range of such widely accepted accounts of the meanings of statements attributing omnipotence, omniscience, and perfect goodness to God.

NON-LITERAL ACCOUNTS OF GOD'S ATTRIBUTES

(a) God as unknowable by us, as being wholly other, wholly transcendent. Quite a number of contemporary writers come very close to the view that God is unknowable by us, that we can know nothing of his attributes, yet there is a general reluctance to state this openly and explicitly. H. L. Mansel, writing during the 19th century in *Limits of Religious Thought* is one who set out this view unequivocally and unashamedly thus:

"It is a fact which experience forces upon us, and which it is useless, were it possible to disguise, that the representation of God after the model of the highest human morality which we are capable of conceiving, is not sufficient to account for all the phenomena exhibited by the course of his natural Providence. The infliction of physical suffering, the permission of moral evil, the adversity of the good, the prosperity of the wicked, the crimes of the guilty involving the misery of the innocent, the tardy appearance and partial distribution of moral and religious knowledge in the world – these are facts which no doubt are reconcilable, we know not why, with the Infinite Goodness of God, but which certainly are not to be explained on the supposition that its sole and sufficient type is to be found in the finite goodness of man." [4]

And, as J. S. Mill noted, Mansel identified with Vulgar Rationalism the view:

". . . that the attributes of God differ from those of man in degree only, not in kind, and hence that certain mental qualities of which we are immediately conscious in ourselves, furnish at the same time a true and adequate image of the infinite perfections of God." [5]

And the further view that:

". . . all the excellences of which we are conscious in the creature, must necessarily exist in the same manner, though in a higher degree, in the Creator. God is indeed more wise, more just, more merciful, than man; but for that very reason, his wisdom and justice and mercy, must contain

[4] Preface to the 4th Edition, p. 13.
[5] *Ibid.,* p. 26.

nothing that is incompatible with the corresponding attributes in their human character." [6]

Mill, commenting on the arguments which lie behind these views, states:

"He (Mansel) maintains the necessary relativity of our knowledge. He holds that the Absolute and the Infinite, or, to use a more significant expression, an Absolute and an Infinite Being, are inconceivable by us; and that when we strive to conceive what is thus inaccessible to our faculties, we fall into self-contradiction. That we are, nevertheless, warranted in believing, and bound to believe, the real existence of an absolute and infinite being, and that this being is God. God, therefore, is inconceivable, and unknowable by us. ... Through this inherent impossibility of our conceiving or knowing God's essential attributes, we are disqualified from judging what is or is not consistent with them. ... This, at least, is the drift of Mr. Mansel's argument; but I am bound to admit that he affirms the conclusion with a certain limitation; for he acknowledges, that the moral character of the doctrines of a religion ought to count for something among the reasons for accepting or rejecting, as of divine origin, the religion as a whole. ... These concessions, however, to the moral feelings of mankind, are made at the expense of Mr. Mansel's logic. If his theory is correct, he has no right to make either of them." [7]

Mill's manner of dealing with this position is to insist that if God is really unknowable, and if "justice", "goodness", "power", etc., when applied to God mean we know not what, then we have no right to use these words. We are entitled to use them only if they mean what they ordinarily mean. What Mill has to say here is an overstatement, but one which rests on an important truth. However, our concern here is with the concept of God and the problem of evil, and not with the question as to whether there exists some being, some or all of whose attributes are unknowable. If the attributes of God are completely unknowable by man, we cannot know that he/it is God, and have no right to call him/it by that name. Further, we should not be entitled to use any attributive words of him/it. It is significant that it is mainly but not only statements about God's moral attributes that Mansel singles out for special mention – it is about these that the theist tends to be most obscurantist. However, Mansel's general argument from the inconceivability of the concept of the essential attributes of God entails that we cannot even know that God is omnipotent, omniscient, perfect in every way. If we cannot know this, we cannot know that we are entitled

---

[6] *Ibid.,* p. 28.

[7] *An Examination of Sir William Hamilton's Philosophy,* 5th edition, London, Longmans, Green, Reader & Dyer, 1878, pp. 111-2.

to postulate that this being is God. To accept a concept of God, we need to have some positive attributes written into the concept. If we have no positive attributes, or if we have merely negative attributes, for example, invisible, intangible, weightless, and the like, all we can say is that we have a concept of nothing, or, more accurately, that we have no concept at all before our minds. If we believe that some being exists but can have no knowledge of its attributes, we have no right to call this being God, and our position would in effect be an agnostic one. Hence we should also be agnostic about whether there is a real problem of evil. God may be omnipotent, or simply be of limited power, wholly or imperfectly good. In the case of the person who worships such a God, we have someone who is prepared to worship an infinite or finite God, a Perfect Being or one who is predominantly evil. Obviously, a serious theist cannot take the view God is *completely* unknowable in respect of his attributes. The difficulties in the way of a theism based on a belief in a finite God will be discussed in the next Chapter.

(b) God as knowable but the knowledge of some or all of his attributes as inexpressible or incommunicable

This kind of view is adopted in varying degrees by many theists, the positions ranging from the extreme one advanced by R. Otto to the very qualified one indicated by T. McPherson.[8] In "Religion as the Inexpressible" McPherson explains:

"Religion belongs to the sphere of the unsayable, so it is not to be wondered at that in theology there is much nonsense (i.e. many absurdities); this is the natural result of trying to put into words – and to discuss – various kinds of inexpressible 'experiences', and of trying to say things about God."

However very soon he qualifies this observing:

"There certainly seems to be this wrong with it, that it may exclude too much: in throwing out the water of theology we may also be throwing out the baby of 'direct', 'first-order' religious assertions; and this we may well not want to do." [9]

In *The Philosophy of Religion* McPherson develops this same general view by reference to literal, semiotic and symbolic meanings, where the

---

[8] R. Otto, *The Idea of the Holy*, London, O.U.P., 1939 and T. McPherson "Religion as the Inexpressible", *New Essays in Philosophical Theology*, London, S.C.M., 1955, pp. 131-143.

[9] *Op. cit.*, p. 142.

expression may have semiotic meaning by way of metaphor or analogy which can be explained, whilst symbolic meaning does not admit of explanation.[10] McPherson notes that this is an idiosyncratic view of symbolic meaning and amounts to his way of noting that religion involves expressions which do not admit of translation, but which seek to express the inexpressible. This is distinct from the symbolic account of C. A. Campbell which will be discussed later in this Chapter. The general view that McPherson entertains is that some religious knowledge is inexpressible or expressible only in language which cannot be translated into language which admits of being literally understood. Those who adopt this kind of view often do so because they believe that the categories and concepts of our language are vastly diferent from those which apply to God.

Many philosophers would wish to deny the possibility of knowledge which cannot be expressed in language. Consider the thought, spirit and inspiration behind logical positivism, with its use of the verification principle. Against this, I should wish to argue for the possibility of knowledge which is in fact inexpressible in language which is to be literally understood. Infants, animals, beings without language, seem to be capable of knowing some things, even though they are incapable of developing a language in which to express this knowledge. With feelings, adults often find that they cannot at all adequately express their love to one another. Words when used literally or even metaphorically seem to distort, render commonplace, even to debase what is a unique, precious feeling, and some are led not to attempt to express the inexpressible, rather than to seek to express what they feel and thereby misreport it. We believe that there is a uniqueness about many feelings, and it is this very uniqueness that gets in the way of accurate expression and not in the way of our knowledge of our unique feeling. If there were an utterly unique being, we should possibly but by no means necessarily be in the same position in respect to it – we may find that we can simply state that we know that it exists but that we cannot express what X is, because the concepts of our language do not apply. With aesthetic appreciation, which I construe as being appreciation of some objective phenomenon in the world, one may be totally unable to express the quality of the music, work of art, which produces the response. One may be quite clear in one's mind but lack the language with which to express it. To a certain extent this is true of certain metaphysical concepts. Whether or not one accepts Plato's theory of forms, it does none the less appear to be a significant theory. Yet the role played in it by the Form of the Good is such that it is the sort of entity which could

[10] London, Van Nostrand, 1965.

be known but not fully reported upon. Plato sought to express this by speaking of it as being beyond knowledge. Thus I wish to argue in the abstract for the possibility of inexpressible, including logically inexpressible, knowledge; that such knowledge is in principle possible. The problem is not whether anyone has or has had such knowledge, but whether such knowledge could conceivably be had of a being called God, and that only such inexpressible knowledge was possible in respect of the major attributes of God which concern us in the context of the problem of evil.

The relevant considerations here can best be brought out by noting the attributes of God as ascribed in orthodox theology. As we have already seen, the notions of omnipotence, and of omniscience, are comparatively straightforward. An omnipotent being is one who has the power to bring about anything that is logically possible. He cannot do what is logically self-contradictory, for example, make square circles, but he can do anything which is logically possible, and cannot be prevented from doing so by any other being. There are some issues which suggest a certain incoherence in the notion of an omnipotent being possessing other perfections, but the notion of an omnipotent being considered as such is clear and coherent enough as was argued earlier in this Chapter. We seem to be able to grasp fully the concept of omnipotence; we are clear that a being cannot be more than omnipotent; and that there cannot be more than one omnipotent being. Thus we can meaningfully and literally assert that God is omnipotent knowing what we mean, just as we know what it is to assert that God or some other being is not omnipotent. An extreme exponent of the inexpressibility thesis would hold that all knowledge of God is inexpressible. Since this is not the case in respect of omnipotence, anyone who holds the inexpressibility view in respect of God's power, must be denying that God is omnipotent, i.e., perfect in respect of power. This would be to accept a finite God. Yet the only logically possible alternative to God being omnipotent, is for him to be finite or limited in power; and this too can be known and expressed literally. The inexpressibility thesis would seem to have no basis in respect of God's power.

The same holds in respect of God's wisdom and knowledge, that is, his omniscience. Omniscience is a readily understood notion, involving as it does the idea of the having of knowledge of all things. Again, if God were said not to be omniscient in a literal sense, then the only alternative would be for him to be limited in respect of knowledge. This notion of limited knowledge also presents no difficulties in respect of literal speech.

It is only in respect of God's goodness that any sort of understanding of this "inexpressibility" thesis as it may relate to the attributes of God central to the problem of evil becomes possible, and then the understanding is more apparent than real. We cannot give any meaning to a being who surpasses omnipotence and omniscience in excellence in respect of power and knowledge, since these are limiting notions, whereas by contrast, the idea of a being surpassing the excellent in respect of morality or goodness is not so immediately absurd. Just as some aestheticians speak of the sublime as surpassing the beautiful, so it has been claimed that there may be an X which surpasses the good in excellence such that we cannot express its excellence. In fact, such a claim involves a very special, questionable view concerning good, that it is indeterminate in the sense of applying to a scale without end, rather than to a determinate scale with an end. Alternatively, it involves the view that there is a scale of goodness and a superior scale of super-goodness, which is of that which is better than good. It implies that significant meaning can be given to better than morally excellent, when in fact, the expression is meaningless. The only respect in which God's moral perfection could surpass a man's moral perfection would be in respect of success and opportunities for successful endeavour; these factors do not make one being morally more excellent or good than another.

Further, it is important to note that if the notion of a superior, inexpressible goodness were significant, it would render the problem of evil even more acute for the theist. A super or supra-moral being would be even less prone to allow evil to exist. That a super-moral being could not be more or less prone to all evil than a perfectly moral being, again brings out the untenability of any claim relating to the inexpressible goodness, that is super- or supra-goodness of God.

More commonly it is claimed that it is statements about God's personal traits, that God is our father, and one who loves us, and wants us lovingly to respond to his love, that would be cited as examples of statements that seek to express the inexpressible. (They are also explained as metaphorical statements, as analogies, and the like). Unfortunately for the theist as will be argued in Chapter 8, the role played by such statements in proposed solutions to the problem of evil is such that treating them as expressions of the inexpressible or even as metaphors or analogies will not do; in respect of God's personal and loving nature, a more literal interpretation is needed by the solutions in which reference is made to these attributes.

(c) God's attributes as knowable and expressible, but not literally

Here we come to the more orthodox as well as to some unorthodox theories. The range of actual theories is great, that of possible theories, limitless.

(i) Religious utterances as metaphorical utterances

For the reasons given above concerning omnipotence and omniscience, it is difficult to see how assertions about God's power and knowledge could be construed as being simply metaphorical and not as literal statements. Indeed, it is difficult to see what sort of metaphorical utterance would be possible here, and how it could be cashed in literal language. It necessarily would have to be cashed in terms of God not being literally all-powerful and all-knowing. Yet if that is so, those who hold this view of God would have no reason for concern about the traditional problem of evil for they would have as their God a finite being, since the only alternative to a being that is literally omnipotent is one who is limited in power. Similarly with omniscience. Again it is difficult to see how this account in terms of metaphorical expression can be applied in respect of God's goodness. If God is good only metaphorically, he would not be good enough literally to be God. In fact, the notion of being metaphorically good appears to be unintelligible. If God is good *qua* moral, rational being, he cannot be called good simply metaphorically. Whilst it is true that some statements about God, for example, that he is a person, a father, and the like, seem to be advanced metaphorically and then used as if they have been advanced literally, these metaphorical statements can be given meaning only on the basis of some literally understood assertions about God. Not all statements about God can be metaphorical. We can speak metaphorically about God as a father only on the basis of God having some of the attributes a father must possess, that is to say, only on the basis of some points of resemblance. In brief, the attempt to explain assertions about God in respect of his power, knowledge, and goodness as metaphors and not as literal truths, cannot succeed, but the attempts to explain such assertions in this way indicates that theists who hold this view are committed to a view of God as being finite and limited.

(ii) Analogy as ordinarily understood

Analogous predication is a whole subject in its own right in theology. At this point I propose to consider only communication by analogy as we ordinarily understand analogy, and later in this Chapter to discuss analogous predication as explained by Thomists in terms of the analogy of proportionality. Analogous predication involves a resemblance which can be literally described. A typical analogy is: Petrol is to car as food is to a human being. Both sides of this analogy can literally be filled out without remainder. So too with analogies concerning God. God is like a father to his creations (simile) is another way of saying that God is to his creations as a father is to his children, (analogy), and these are statements which admit of further specification. One can properly demand to be told the basis of the similarity and look and see whether it is correctly reported. This suggests that analogy is not a basic mode of communication but a short-cut or dramatic way of communicating what can be communicated literally. Thus I suggest that talk about analogous predication will not be the job required in respect of omnipotence, omniscience and goodness, and that it too if used in reference to these attributes would involve an acceptance of a finite, limited, imperfect God. Further, as will be argued later, the attempt to explain statements to the effect that God is a father, a person, a being capable of love for his creations as analogies, would render the attributes referred to and so explained, too remote from the attributes literally referred to by these expressions, for the former to bear the burden they are required to bear in proposed solutions to the problem of evil.

(iii) Knowledge and communication by models

I. Ramsey approaches this kind of theory by distinguishing three types of attributes and characterizations of God as follows: Attributes of negative theology such as immutable, impassible; characterization of God by unity, simplicity, perfection; and the ascription of other traditionally acknowledged attributes such as *First* Cause, *infinitely* wise, *infinitely* good, eternal purpose. It is in respect of the third group that his account of models and qualifiers emerges most clearly. In respect of the first group Ramsey observes:

"So when we talk of God as 'immutable', or as 'impassible', the function of these particular attribute-words is primarily to evoke the kind of situation we have just been mentioning; to fix on mutable and passible features of perceptual situations and to develop these features in such a way that there is evoked a characteristically different situation which is the foundation *in fact* for assertions about God's immutability or impassibility . . .

"For these words 'immutability' and 'impassibility' make also a *language* plea. They claim for the word 'God' a position outside of all mutable and passible language. Beyond that negative claim the attributes of negative theology do not however go. All they tell us is that if anything is 'mutable' it will not be exact currency for God; that if anything is 'passible' it will not be exact currency for God. So the main merit of attribute words like 'immutable' and 'impassible' is to give a kind of technique for meditation; their main merit is evocative." [11]

And:

"We have seen that 'God is impassible', like 'God is immutable', is to be understood by its ability to evoke in terms of 'passibility' stories what we have called the characteristic theological situation. Further, when the light dawns and the penny drops, to say that 'God is impassible' is to claim that the word 'God' is a word which cannot be confined to passibility language. In other words, this first assertion concentrates on evoking the fact and claiming that 'God' is nothing if not logically odd." [12]

All this is unilluminating. In respect of the attributes of unity, simplicity, perfection, if the former may be called such, Ramsey suggests that these words make use of the methods of contrasts, we approaching the meaning of unity by reflection about diversity, simplicity by reflection about complexity. We are said to reflect on diversity and on how it may be thought of as a unity – furniture and rooms in one house; many houses in one city, until "at some point or other the penny drops, the light dawns, and there is a characteristic 'disclosure' and there is evoked that situation in relation to which the word 'unity' is to be commended." [13] Again this is unhelpful. With many "the penny does not drop"; and with those for whom it does, different disclosures are to be reported.

With other attributes, and these it would appear include those with which we are most concerned in the context of the problem of evil, namely omnipotence, omniscience, and perfect goodness, Ramsey illustrates his account by reference to *First* Cause and *infinitely* good. Here Ramsey explains that first is the qualifier, a directive which prescribes a special way

---

[11] I. Ramsey, *Religious Language*, London, S.C.M., 1957, pp. 52-3. See also "Paradox in Religion", *Aristotelian Society Supplementary Volume*, XXXIII, 1959.
[12] *Ibid.*, p. 89.
[13] *Ibid.*, p. 54.

of developing those "model" situations; "first" presses us backward and backward; at some point there is "a sense of the unseen", when the light dawns, the penny drops, the ice breaks. And when "*First* cause" leads us to posit "God" according to the procedure we have been describing, it claims at the same time that the word "God" completes causal stories, and is "logically prior" to such stories.[14]

Of "*infinitely* good", Ramsey writes that he is concerned to refute the suggestion that "infinitely good" is a meaningless phrase. The word 'infinite' is said to have two logical functions – to stimulate us to develop stories of good lives in the right direction and also to point to something outside "good" language altogether.[15]

Later on in the book Ramsey considers "God is loving" and argues that this expression claims:

"That we can model God in terms of 'loving' situations ... but as it stands the assertion is logically incomplete in an important way, and that to avoid this incompletion we ought to insert some appropriate qualifier such as 'infinitely' or 'all'." [16]

This is simply a restatement of the problem. If God does not literally love his creations, what then it may be asked, is the sense in which the word "love" is used. The suggestion that the qualification "infinite" alters the meaning from a literal to a non-literal one which we come to understand by means of a disclosure will not do. The talk of disclosure is vague and unsatisfactory. It is true that people do sometimes think that they gain insights from paradoxes, parables, models, and the like, but different people think that they get different insights from the same models, and not all can be right, or rather, not all can be of the real God nor of the God of orthodox theology which is presupposed in the acceptance of the problem of evil as even an apparent problem. We need therefore to know what is the right way to construe a model and a qualifier so that we gain a true insight into God's nature. This Ramsey is unable to tell us. Thus I suggest that the following disjunctive conclusion is to be drawn: Either the theory of models and qualifiers is another variety of obscurantism which leaves us totally uninformed as to the attributes of God, and in particular, whether he is literally a perfect being, or simply a finite God, or Ramsey's is a subjectivist theory which renders the attributes of God to be subjectively determined, and dependent on the particular individual concerned and on his personal disclosures, these varying from individual to individual.

[14] *Ibid.*, pp. 62-3.
[15] *Ibid.*, pp. 75-80.
[16] *Ibid.*, p. 98.

In either event, Ramsey's account leaves us in ignorance as to whether God is a being of a kind that would give rise to the traditional problem of evil, or whether he is a finite, limited, imperfect being who is not a fitting object of religious worship.

(iv) Campbell's symbolic account

Campbell's account here is of particular interest, as few contemporary theists have taken the problem of evil more seriously than Campbell. Yet in his account of the attributes of God, Campbell so explains God as to make this concern with the problem surprising. Campbell here observes:

"Let us turn now to the symbols that are our especial business; those rational concepts like Power, Value, Love, Justice, Wisdom, Mercy, and Personality which theistic religions almost all predicate of God in some sense, and which supra-rational theism insists ought to be regarded, and can significantly be regarded, as *symbols only* of a God whose ultimate nature transcends human powers of conception." [17]

He then goes on to argue later concerning our knowledge of the attributes of God:

"Theism in general, it will be recalled, we took to be sufficiently defined as belief in one God, an Eternal and Infinite Spirit, Perfect in power, wisdom and goodness, who is the ultimate source of all that is, who is the Moral Governor of the world, and who is yet a Living Presence in the hearts of men. Supra-rational theism (with which we are now alone concerned) we distinguished from Rational Theism in virtue of its insistence that the Divine nature transcends all possible human conception, and that while the qualities Rational Theism ascribes to God are truly ascribable, they are so only when understood in a symbolic significance." [18]

And:

"The solution of the dilemma I take to be as follows. The propositions which affirm respectively unity, infinitude, and eternity of the ultimately real have each a negative as well as a positive aspect. In each we intend to deny something of the real, and we also intend to affirm of it some positive content. What I suggest is that these propositions are literally true in respect of what they *deny,* but only symbolically true in respect of what they *affirm.*" [19]

[17] C. A. Campbell, *Selfhood and Godhood*, p. 351. See also pp. 349-350 for Campbell's account of a "symbol".
[18] *Ibid.*, p. 404.
[19] *Ibid.*, p. 406.

And:

"And now what of the further characterisation of God as a Spirit, perfect in goodness, wisdom and power? Is corroboration from our philosophical standpoint possible here too? I think that it is – always bearing in mind that the religion we are concerned to corroborate claims no more than a symbolic significance for the ascription of these characters to God." [20]

Again this is an account of God's attributes as not being what a literal interpretation of the words used would suggest. It also implies that the attributes could be stated in terms of expressions which are to be interpreted literally. This follows from the notion of a symbol. For something to be a symbol, it must symbolize something; and we must know how it symbolizes that for which it stands. We need therefore direct awareness of the object or bearer of the symbol in its literal form. Consider here a symbol such as that of the Cross. What it symbolizes can be expressed in literal terms. Thus in rejecting the literal interpretation of God's power, wisdom and goodness, Campbell implies that God is not literally the possessor of these attributes. (There are some complex qualifications concerning the moral law and goodness later in his discussion). Hence on his view, there would seem to be no problem of evil. Campbell in fact in his account of symbolism takes the view that we may know something to be a symbol of something else, without being able to express what we know, or even to know all, of that for which the symbol stands. To that extent his view becomes closer to the inexpressibility thesis examined earlier in this Chapter.

(v) Analogous predication [21]

In Thomistic philosophy, analogy figures as a large subject in its own right. Many different senses of analogy are distinguished, but only one of these senses is important to our problem of the meaning of assertions ascribing attributes to God. Aquinas's discussion in *Summa Contra Gentiles* is brief, as is that in *Summa Theologiae*. Mascall's account is thorough, that of McInerny detailed. However the brief, lucid discussion of Copleston is adequate for our purposes.

[20] *Ibid.,* p. 407.
[21] See Aquinas, *Summa Theologiae*, I, 8, 5c, *Summa Contra Gentiles*, I, 34; E. L. Mascall, *Existence and Analogy*, London, Longmans, Green, 1949; R. M. McInerny, *The Logic of Analogy*, The Hague, Martinus Nijhoff, 1961; and F. Copleston: *Aquinas*, Harmondsworth, Penguin, 1955.

It is impossible to gain a clear conception of God by reference merely to negative terms. Equally, it is not possible to explain the ascription of positive attributes to God in terms of God being the cause of them in man. To say that God is wise, or that he is healthy, in the sense that he is the cause of wisdom or of health in men is to leave the hearer without a clear grasp of the attributes of God. As Copleston points out, if God is good only in the sense parallel to that in which he can be said to be corporeal, he would be no more literally good than he is literally corporeal. This leads to the doctrine of analogous predication. The sense in which terms such as wisdom, goodness, and power are said to be analogously predicated of God is to be distinguished from equivocal, metaphorical, and simple analogous uses of the words involved. The sense of analogy that is relevant here is that of analogy of proportionality. In the modern context, this is a misleading name. Analogy of proportionality relates to attributes which are known as pure perfections, that is, to attributes the possession of which involves no limitation in the possessor. Compare here attributes such as power, wisdom, and intelligence on the one hand, and corporeality and being a person on the other. We derive our knowledge of the pure perfections from things in this world but can none the less attribute them to God. In so attributing them to God we are using these expressions in a more primary sense. Thus Aquinas wrote:

"*I answer that,* According to the preceding article, our knowledge of God is derived from the perfections which flow from Him to creatures, which perfections are in God in a more eminent way than in creatures. Now our intellect apprehends them as they are in creatures, and as it apprehends them it signifies them by names. Therefore as to the names applied to God, there are two things to be considered – *viz.,* the perfections which they signify, such as goodness, life, and the like, and their mode of signification. As regards what is signified by these names, they belong properly to God, and more properly than they belong to creatures, and are applied primarily to Him. But as regards their mode of signification, they do not properly and strictly apply to God; their mode of signification applies to creatures." [22]

Copleston explains that from psychological and linguistic points of view, a word like intelligence denotes primarily human intelligence, the intelligence of which we have experience. When it is predicated of God, it is predicated of him from a metaphysical view. Psychologically we come to know intelligence from human beings; we gain a grasp of the English expression by reference to human intelligence. Yet metaphysically

[22] *Summa Theologiae,* I, 13, 3. See also Mascall, *Existence and Analogy.*

it is God to which intelligence is said primarily to apply. This theory is linked with the view that in God there are not distinct attributes but that we can only come to know God piecemeal. This greatly complicates the theory.

By contrast with the accounts so far examined, this account seeks to insist that in some real sense God is omnipotent, omniscient, good, etc., and it is therefore less evidently exposed to the charge of explaining God as being a limited, finite, imperfect being. None the less, it too is exposed to difficulties, including one related to this. Firstly, this kind of predication (and knowledge of the attributes which make up the concept of God) presuppose some knowledge of God in some more direct, literal way. Otherwise we should know only that something existed, we should not know what attributes apply to that which exists. Secondly, it might be argued that these expressions are being used in different senses, that is, slightly equivocally. Consider the commonly used example of life. I am unclear about the word/concept life when we attribute life to trees, animals, men and God. It is by no means clear that when we attribute life to a tree we are using the word in the same sense as when we attribute it to God. With attributes such as power, wisdom, and intelligence, there is a much weaker case for this claim, and these expressions, unlike life, seem to be used in strictly univocal ways. As we have seen, each can be defined in a clear, unequivocal sense such that we can meaningfully ascribe power, wisdom, and intelligence to beings of different types without the concept changing with the category of being to which it is applied. So too with moral goodness, and goodness generally. We should not be using such expressions analogously nor equivocally but in strictly univocal, uniform senses when, on discovering rational, free Martians, or Dolphins which have a language, and who rationally order their lives, in consultation with each other, we ascribe moral goodness or badness to their actions, and goodness to their planned self-perfections. The force of Kant's argument in his *Grundlegung zur Metaphysik der Sitten* consists precisely in this claim in respect of moral goodness. Thirdly, if the senses of these terms are truly different when applied to different categories of being, then, as Copleston concedes, this introduces an element of agnosticism into our knowledge of the nature of God. We should not know what we are really ascribing to God. Further, in respect of attributes such as being a person or having a personal, loving nature, that is, in respect of attributes which involve limitations, and which therefore are not pure perfections, this account would not apply. God either is literally or non-literally a person who loves mankind. The former can be ruled out, since a person cannot be an infinite being. Similarly love must be confined within some bounds. It cannot embrace all beings. This tells not at all against Aquinas's account of analogous predication in respect of pure perfections; but it does reveal the need for a supplementary theory of predication if attributes such as those of being a loving, personal God are to play the roles they play in so many proposed solutions, including many of those offered by Thomists.

The importance of this theory in the context of the problem of evil lies in the element of agnosticism concerning the attributes of God it would introduce if true. To the extent that God is wise, all-knowing, powerful, good, in senses we do not understand, to that extent we cannot be certain how or whether evil creates even a *prima facie* problem for theists who hold this view about God's attributes. Equally, it cannot be known with certainty whether this God is a fitting object of worship. However, I suggest that the basic objection to the theory is that it is not a true account of the predication of the pure perfections, that if they apply to God they apply literally and univocally.

GOD AS A PERSON: HIS PERSONAL TRAITS

It is often argued that God is either literally or metaphorically a person, possessing various personal traits. These claims need to be considered here as various proposed solutions to the problem of evil presuppose that God possesses these personal traits in a literal or in something more akin to a literal sense than to a metaphorical sense.

If the features possessed by persons are listed, and we consider them with a view to determining which might be absent and yet the being still be a person, it is clear that God could not literally be a person nor literally possess personal traits without ceasing to be all-powerful and unlimited in perfection. Among the features of persons *qua* persons are: Life, individuality in the sense of being separate, distinct individuals, with distinctive traits and personalities which mark off one individual from another; all persons, as a contingent fact, other than God if he is a person, are human beings; personal identity – sameness in the person; reason and will; self-consciousness; sentience; i.e., capacity for pain and pleasure, and a capacity to experience feelings such as love, grief, anger, indignation; a capacity to desire and to feel satisfied or thwarted; perception in the sense of being capable of perceiving objects. If there were no perceptual powers at all, we should not be prepared to call the being a person.

We can now consider which of these features could be absent and the being remain a person. I suggest that of the above, the only features are those indicated as being purely contingent ones, namely those relating to persons (other than God, if he is a person) being human beings, possessed of human physical characteristics, such as two legs, arms, and the like. Individuals would differ concerning the standards of self-sameness, and of personal identity which have to be met, and we should not be insistent that a person be capable of experiencing the full range of desires and emotions. Yet many of the features which appear to be essential features are such as would involve limitations which would count as imperfections in an infinite being, and indeed are incompatible with a being, being infinite in all respects.

It is relevant to note here that McTaggart offered an argument directed at attempting to show that God could not be a person. The argument runs: Being a person involves consciousness, self-consciousness. Self-consciousness involves consciousness of an Other. And:

"The more vivid, definite, and extensive is our recognition of the Other, the more vivid and definite becomes our self-consciousness. As consciousness of an Other becomes vague and indefinite, consciousness of self becomes vague and indefinite too. As we fall asleep the two become gradually faint together, and as we awake the two gradually revive together.

An omnipotent person, if one can exist, must be capable of being in a different position from this. He must be capable of existing out of relation to anything except himself . . .

But it is necessary that he should be capable of existing out of all relation to an Other, if he is to be omnipotent. For, if he were not, then he could only be a person on condition that a universe had arisen or would some day arise. That is to say, it would be impossible for him to prevent the existence, some time or other, of a universe." [23]

If it is the case that God cannot be literally a person nor possess personal traits, the question arises as to what is being asserted when it is claimed that he is a person, a father to his creations, who has a personal love and concern for his creations. How can an omnipotent, unlimited being enter into anything *like* those personal relationships which depend on the above-noted personal traits. In so far as the relationship is one which can properly be said to be *like* a personal one, it would to that extent involve limitations. How can a being incapable of experiencing suffering, grief, fear, and the like, enter into a personal relation with a grief-stricken, fearful person? There are obvious difficulties in the way of accounts in

[23] J. McT. E. McTaggart, *Some Dogmas of Religion,* London, Edward Arnold, 1930, p. 205.

terms of metaphors, similes, and analogies, for they admit of the question and a demand for an answer concerning the basis of the figurative use of language, an answer in terms of real and describable likenesses.

LOVE

There are special problems with love. The *Concise Oxford Dictionary* explains the verb, to love, as meaning: "Hold dear, bear love to, be in love with, be fond of; be in love, cling to, delight in, enjoy having, be addicted to, admire or be glad of the existence of, (life, honour, comfort, gold, *doing,* virtue, man who knows his own mind . . .)." Examples include love of children, of works of art, friends, games. It is usual to distinguish *eros* from *agape*. The question relevant here is whether this sort of love is compatible with divine perfection. Such love involves a caring for, being concerned with and for the loved one, grief at their being hurt or harmed, sorrow at their weaknesses and faults. The concern is not simply intellectual concern but necessarily involves emotional content. The father who despises his son but who exerts himself to the best of his ability on his behalf could not be said to love him. Nor could a father who expressed great concern for his son's welfare, but who did not grieve at all at his son's misfortunes. Kant was fully aware of this, and this is why he argued that we cannot have a duty to love our fellow men, only to act well towards them. This is because love has an emotional content and is not merely a matter of intellectual concern. Emotional concern involves limitations of many kinds. Hence God cannot love his creations in any literal sense; yet any non-literal interpretation which is compatible with God's other attributes seems not to be adequate to the role to which theists put it in their proposed solutions.

In brief, the problem again resolves itself into that concerning how any serious meaning can be given to the claim that God loves his creations. The more remote from the literal meaning it is, the less justification there is for making the claim in this language; the nearer to the literal meaning, the more justification there is for claiming that this contention involves the view that God is finite, limited, imperfect.

CHAPTER V

GOD AS FINITE AND IMPERFECT:
WORSHIPWORTHINESS

It is commonly argued that one way of avoiding the problem of evil is to contend that God is finite, imperfect either in respect of power or goodness. Here it will be argued that this *may be* but need not be the case, that whether or not problems resulting from evil arise for an exponent of this form of theism depends on the details of the account given of God's power and goodness, and on the nature and extent of actual evil.

There are serious difficulties in the way of arguing for the existence of such a being. What arguments there are, for example J. S. Mill's curious and tentative restatement of the argument from design, are singularly unconvincing.[1] There are also good reasons for believing that a finite God would not be a fitting and proper object of religious adoration and worship. None the less a brief discussion of this variety of theism is of the greatest importance because so many theists, in explaining the attributing to God of omnipotence, omniscience, and goodness, deny that these attributes hold literally of God, and hence commit themselves to a belief in a finite, limited, imperfect God.

GOD AS FINITE IN POWER

Clearly, if God is limited in power, the traditional problem of evil stated in the form of Problems 1, 2 and 3 in Chapter 1 will not arise. Further, because such a finite god may be wholly good, and his intentions morally irreproachable, the existence of evil would in no way, it would seem at first glance at least, tell against his existence. All existent evil would be explained as being unavoidable, as resulting from the limitations in God's power. This is how many have argued in urging that this form of theism provides a means of escape from the problem of evil.

[1] *Theism,* originally published in *Three Essays on Religion,* London, Longmans, Green, Reader & Dyer, 1874.

This, I suggest, gives an oversimplified picture of the situation. It is true that the traditional problems of evil do not arise for the person who believes in the existence of a finite God. None the less, evil gives rise to a problem of evil for such a theist, namely the logical problem of showing that there is no self-contradiction involved in asserting that a God who created the world and who is finite in power but wholly good exists, and that evil exists. (This is parallel to the traditional Problem 2 noted in Chapter 1.) It is possible, as Mill noted, that some of the evil which occurs, could have been prevented or avoided by the finite God. Hence, anyone adopting this form of theism will need to show, as do more orthodox theists, that the evil which actually occurs is unavoidable and/or justified in terms of some good or goods.

It is probably because of the difficulty of setting out the atheist case in detail here that it has so commonly been assumed that there is no problem of evil for the theist who believes in the existence of a finite God. Obviously, unless the limitations on his power are precisely indicated, it would be virtually impossible to start an inquiry into whether the known existent evil is or is not avoidable for a finite God. Clearly the theist could simply add more and more limitations to the power of his God if pressed. However, once the amount of power is specified, the problem admits in principle of theoretical statement and examination, and of actual discussion and argument.

There are two other considerations which are relevant to religious belief in such a God, namely, the difficulty in setting out adequate reasons for such a belief, and adequate reasons for worshipping him.

The cosmological and ontological arguments, involving as they do, reference to a necessary being, would seem not to be available to one who believes God to be finite. It is true that it might be argued that a necessary being, in the sense of a non-dependent being, and also in the sense of a being that *must* exist, may be finite in power, but to begin to show this would take the greatest ingenuity of a philosophical genius. The teleological argument, in its usual form, namely as an argument by analogy, would seem to be more plausible as an argument for the existence of a finite God than for that of an all-powerful God. The latter conclusion, as Kant noted, goes beyond what is justified by the premises. However, the fact of evil makes it a question-begging argument if directed at proving the existence of an all-good being of finite power. So too, if faith is explained as it often is, as by Tillich, as the state of being ultimately concerned, as claiming truth for its concern, and as involving commitment, courage, and the taking of a risk, then belief in a finite God based on such faith would seem singularly inappropriate.[2] These considerations are mentioned only to indicate that there are difficulties in the way of grounding such a belief. It is not my purpose here to examine and assess the case for and against a belief in a finite God.

My object is to show that whilst there may remain a problem of evil for the believer in a finite God, there is unavoidably another problem confronting such a theist, namely that concerning the worshipworthiness of such a God, the problem of showing that such a being could be and is a fitting object of religious worship, involving as it does, adoration, blind obedience, and reverence. This is an issue I have discussed more fully in "Would Any Being Merit Worship?".[3] There I argued (i) that it is proper to raise the question of the worshipworthiness of a being, and (ii) that a God limited in power is not a proper object of religious worship. A. C. MacIntyre, in a remarkable discussion in a review of C. B. Martin's *Religious Belief* observed:

"Mr. Martin sometimes writes as if one could establish what is and what is not worthy of religious awe outside the context of a particular religion and a particular theology." [4]

That one can establish what is and what is not worthy of religious awe outside the context of a particular religion and a particular theology is made evident by reflection about the inappropriateness of anyone worshipping a tree which his religion and theology explain as being a tree and nothing more than a tree. Clearly it is not simply inappropriate but wrong for anyone to engage in the religious worship of another person, to hold him in awe, to reverence, adore and wholly to yield his will to that of the other person in religious adoration, and this because ordinary persons are not fitting objects of worship.

The reason it is inappropriate for us to worship other human persons bears on the difficulties in the way of making out a case for showing the worshipworthiness of a finite being. A God whose best may be very bad, whose creations may get out of control, and the like, seems hardly one which can properly be adored. Nor is such a being one to whom it is fitting that we submit ourselves without reservation or qualification. Further, he could not provide the serene confidence, which as C. A. Campbell observes, is an aspect of the worshipful attitude.[5] Findlay argues to the same end:

---

[2] *The Dynamics of Faith.*
[3] *The Southern Journal of Philosophy,* 2, 1964, pp. 157-164.
[4] *Philosophical Quarterly,* 12, 1962, p. 288.
[5] *Op. cit.,* pp. 290-1.

"To feel religiously is therefore to presume surpassing greatness in some object: so much characterises the attitudes in which we bow and bend the knee, and enter into the ordinary meanings of the word 'religious' . . . and ask whether it isn't wholly anomalous to worship anything *limited* in any thinkable manner. For all limited superiorities are tainted with an obvious relativity, and can be dwarfed in thought by still mightier superiorities, in which process of being dwarfed they lose their claim upon our worshipful attitudes. And hence we are led on irresistibly to demand that our religious object should have an unsurpassable supremacy along all avenues, that it should tower infinitely above all other objects." [6]

It is relevant here that a belief in the existence of a finite God may be and in fact has been associated with a belief in the existence of another being or other beings, usually an evil being or evil beings. One could reasonably adopt an attitude of respect and cooperation towards such a finite, good God, but to worship him in the full sense of worship, would be to act inappropriately, and indeed, wrongly.

AN OMNIPOTENT GOD WHO IS MORALLY IMPERFECT

The traditional problem of evil arises from the demand that God must be shown to be wholly good. Hence any view according to which God is morally imperfect, which proceeds by dealing with the problem of evil by acknowledging that God knowingly and willingly allows or causes avoidable, unjustified, evil does so by denying a major premise of the problem, and hence the problem. It is true that a person may be prepared to entertain the view that a morally imperfect being is God – for example if the moral blemishes were few and the being good overall. Mill entertained this possibility as a serious one. I suggest that the difficulty into which this approach runs is in respect of a challenge to the premise, if God is explained as a being who must be a fitting object of religious worship. To worship, revere, adore, and to yield our wills to a being who may do evil or permit evil which we ourselves should feel morally obliged to prevent if we could, is to act in a morally irresponsible way, it is to abandon our moral autonomy in favour of a being we know to be capable of immoral acts. Further, on the human plane, we see that there are limits to the respect we can attribute to a human being who occasionally acts in an immoral way.

The position is none the less of interest for the reasons indicated in the

---

[6] "Can God's Existence Be Disproved?" in *New Essays in Philosophical Theology,* ed. A. Flew and A. MacIntyre, p. 51.

previous Chapter, namely, that by seeking to explain the omnipotence, omniscience, and goodness of God as holding not literally but in some non-literal sense, a great many theists come in their explanations of the nature of God to adopt, albeit unwittingly, a position not very different, if different at all, from this. Consider here Mansel's account.

A GOD IMPERFECT BOTH IN POWER AND GOODNESS

A theist may be prepared to entertain the view that a being may be God even though he be limited both in power and goodness. Mill did not dismiss such a position as absurd. Historically, many theists have worshipped such gods – consider the Homeric gods, the gods of primitive religions, and the like. The reason such religions are not treated seriously by philosophers today is because of the considerations indicated above. This form of theism need occupy us no longer.

THE WORSHIPWORTHINESS OF AN OMNIPOTENT, OMNISCIENT, GOOD GOD

This Chapter has been concerned, among other things, with the issue of the worshipworthiness of a God limited in power, or in goodness, or in both. It may be thought from this discussion that the writer accepts the view that an all-perfect God is a worshipworthy being. This does not necessarily follow. There are difficulties in the way of justifying wholly yielding one's will to another, no matter how perfect; and there are problems of the kind noted in Chapter 4 of reconciling the various perfections of the so-called perfect being, such that there may be grounds for withholding worship in the fullest sense of worship. Consider the paradox arising from God's omnipotence and his goodness. Consider also the paradox that arises from the fact that his goodness is either contingent, and hence not certain, or necessary, and not really goodness.

CHAPTER VI

MUST A WORLD CREATED BY AN ALL-PERFECT BEING BE WHOLLY FREE OF EVIL?

The traditional problem of evil is of the form that the existence of *any* evil creates a problem in respect of the perfection of God – consider again the various statements of the problem of evil set out in Chapter 1. Yet, if the discussion in Chapter 2 establishes anything, it establishes that if there is a God, he did not create a world entirely free of evil. Thus our substantial question in this Chapter consists in examining the assumption underlying the statement of the traditional problem of evil, namely that there is at least a *prima facie* incompatibility between the existence of a perfect God and the existence of *any* evil. Our question may therefore be stated in the form, 'Ought or must a perfect being make a world which is wholly good, wholly free of evil?' Theists who discuss this problem usually answer it in the negative, citing by way of support of their contention, examples of men justifiably causing evil that good may come. A more fundamental line of questioning is that of M. B. Ahern who argues that it has not been shown, and that it cannot be shown, that there is an analytic ethical principle, which would provide the essential connecting link between the assertions: This world contains evil; this world was created by a wholly good, omnipotent, omniscient being: if a self-contradiction between the assertions is to be established.[1] Ahern argues that those who have insisted that there is a problem have in fact set out ethical principles which involve explicit or implicit reference to the amount or kinds of evil, for example, to the evil being excessive and hence unjustified or avoidable, or they have simply set out as the connecting principle, false ethical principles which are synthetic propositions, and not 'true' analytic propositions as required in the detailed statement of the traditional problem. As Ahern supports his contention by reference to examples both of justified evils and of principles set out by those who claim that evil, any evil, is a real problem for the theist, we may first consider the argument from examples of justifiable evils.

[1] *Op. cit.*, Chapter 3.

The theist's claim is that if it is shown that some evil, no matter how little evil, can be justified by reference to good, the traditional problem concerning the existence of some evil (Problem 1) ceases to be a problem. The problem then becomes the different problem, namely whether the actual evil occurs is justified (Problem 2).

The Surgeon Model. One kind of example theists (but not Ahern who rightly rejects it as irrelevant) like to use is that of the surgeon or dentist who inflicts pain as a means of bringing health, or in order to bring relief from pain or suffering. The actions of surgeons and dentists are in no way morally wrong. The added evil of the pain of the operation or extraction, over and above the evils of ill-health and the pain, suffering, or discomfort involved, is justified by the good it brings or the evil it eliminates. This is true. However, it is not true that whenever evil means result in greater good or less evil, they are morally justified. Whether we judge them to be justified or not, depends on the nature of the evils and goods, on whether the goods could have been achieved without the evil means and by means which are wholly good, and more basically, on whether one's normative ethic is essentially a utilitarian one, and utilitarianism a tenable ethic.

The relevance of the nature of goods and evils: In the case of the surgeon, the evil he inflicts is usually of the kind he seeks to prevent, namely pain or the loss of an organ, a capacity, life itself, and in most cases suffering. In most cases he artificially (in spite of anaesthetics, there are post-operative pains) brings some pain into being as a means to or as a side effect of his means of preventing greater pain (or serious loss of organs and capacities with consequent pain and/or suffering). Thus typically the surgeon causes pain in order to avoid greater evils in the forms of greater pain, suffering, and/or death. The typical cases of surgery are therefore not models to which the theist can appeal because they seek to provide by reference to the surgeon a justification of all evil, when in fact most surgery is justified not as a means to goods, but as means to lessening or postponing evils. There is still evil to be justified.

It is true that a person may be willing to suffer the pain involved in an operation, not to avoid an evil, but to gain increased pleasure in the long run. Some plastic surgery, that is, surgery which is now called cosmetic surgery sought by already beautiful women may be of this kind. Yet it is questionable whether even cosmetic surgery provides a completely appropriate model. We should not regard ourselves as being morally justified in coercing anyone into having cosmetic surgery to increase their pleasure or happiness against their wills. Indeed, we are reluctant to coerce those who need operations to lessen their pain and suffering or even to save their lives. To drug a person and then have him operated upon in order to terminate his pain or to save his life, is to act in a way most people would regard as indefensible if the individual concerned were a mature, intelligent, albeit cowardly adult. Yet such surgery would seem to be nearer to being the model the theist needs to provide a justification of physical evil in this world.

Yet even such a model is not completely apt. The model which is really relevant is that of the surgeon who operates on one – removing a kidney or cornea, or both kidneys and both corneas – in order to transplant them in another or others, and this against the wishes of the donor. This is the kind of evil to be found in the world; this is the kind of evil which needs to be justified. If under the description of "some or any evil" this kind of evil may fall, obviously it will not be justified merely as a means.

The foregoing argument is directed at showing that: (i) If evil is shown to admit of justification as a means of lessening evil, then the theist has not shown by reference to the surgeon model that evil can always be justified as a means; (ii) that the kind of evil involved as a means to goods is relevant to whether it can be justified. Thus a blanket justification of any/some evil in terms of its being a means to goods is not possible along these lines. The strongest conclusion the theist can draw is that some/any evil *may* admit of justification along these lines – it all depends on the kind of evil that makes up the some/any evil. To this it may be replied that this is still to argue by reference to actual evil or evil which may be actual and not to evil in the sense say of a minor evil such as a toothache, as constituting the evil in "some evil." More argument is needed.

Such argument is available in the form of the more basic objection made by McTaggart and others, namely that to use an intrinsically evil means to achieve an end when the end could be achieved without the evil means is to act evilly, given that no loss of goods and no new evils occur as a result of bringing about the end directly. Thus, for a dentist to extract teeth without using an anaesthetic when it could easily be used, would be for the dentist to act in an evil way. Similarly, for legislators to seek to raise the standard of living in an under-developed country by killing off half the population, when the standard of living of the remaining half could be raised as easily by improved agricultural methods, would be abominably evil. We countenance the use of evil means only when good means are not available. This fact is very relevant to the theistic situation. An omnipotent God is able to achieve all the goods directly, without using means, which in the human situation require on occasion, evil means, and this because of the limitations of human power. The attempt to show that evil may be justified by reference to goods to which it is or may be a means therefore fails.

Awareness of this fact has led many theists to argue that evil may be justified in other ways and not simply as means to goods. Evil may be justified as a necessary by-product of a mode of securing goods, or it may be an essential condition for attaining goods in the sense of goods not capable of coming into being without the evils. These are distinct contentions and need to be examined separately.

A simple example of an evil which is a by-product of a good, and which is accepted as being an evil we are justified as bringing into being because of the value of the goods involved is, until recently at least, the pollution caused by the motor car. Men, until now at least, had to accept the package-deal, car and the goods it brings into being and the evils it prevents, plus the pollution, or no car and its goods and the evils it prevents, and no car-caused pollution. Another example would be that of organic existence, for example, existence as a living human being which involves by-products which, if not evils, are disvalued. If an attempt is made to suggest that a solution to the traditional problem of evil is possible along these lines, that evil may be justified as a necessary by-product of means to goods, or of the existence of goods, better examples are required, for the necessity here is *empirical* necessity. What is required is a model example of evils which are *logically* consequent on the goods or the means of achieving them. There do seem to be examples available, although Maritain, in his talk about the necessity of some, among corruptible beings, being corrupted, claims that organic life itself provides such an example. In this context Maritain writes:

" 'Perfection of the universe', St. Thomas continues, 'requires therefore that there be some beings who can fall from goodness; and if there are beings who can fall from goodness, the result will be that such defection will in fact sometimes occur in those beings'. For if it is in the nature of things that an event can happen, this event actually will happen sometimes." [2]

Maritain here is treating of human freedom but what he claims is evidently intended to apply to corruptibles generally. For this reason his later claim, made also in *God and the Permission of Evil*,[3] is also relevant. He claims:

"God, therefore, cannot make any creature who is naturally impeccable,

---

[2] *St. Thomas and the Problem of Evil*, Milwaukee, Marquette University Press, 1942, p. 6.

[3] Milwaukee, Bruce, 1966, pp. 37 ff.

any more than He can make a squared circle; these are not necessities independent of God . . .; these necessities themselves depend on His very
essence as His intelligence sees it, seeing at the same time all those ways
in which that very essence can be participated in." [4]

I suggest that Maritain is obviously in error both in respect of corruptibles who lack free will and those who possess it. Failure is not a logical
necessity, simply an empirical fact. To suggest that God cannot make
corruptibles who are not corrupted is seriously to limit his power.

A more plausible example is that cited by M. B. Ahern, namely that of
a married couple who decide to have a child knowing that it will suffer
evils – childhood diseases, pain, and in later life, suffering. They know too
that the person they plan to bring into being will do morally evil acts. As
Ahern has noted, this example can be generalized – all physical evils affect-
ing human beings and all moral evil could be terminated by terminating
the human race, for example, by all refraining from reproduction; yet few
would think that the prevention of the evils justified the elimination of the
goods involved. Plausible as are these examples, I suggest that they will
not do. Firstly, if parents *knew* that the evils would outweigh the goods,
for example, if they knew that their child would be mentally and physically
defective, they would not be justified in bringing it into being. So too in
respect of the human race. Further, the human model will not do, for an
omnipotent being could prevent all the physical evils, and, it will be argued
later, cause only those who will be morally good to come into being. (See
Chapter 8, Section B).

Another line of argument consists in claiming that certain goods are
logically dependent on the existence of certain evils, that without the evils
the goods logically could not exist. (This view, which amounts to the claim
that certain goods, the highest goods according to some, are logically parasitic on certain evils, is commonly advanced, paradoxically enough by
many who hold the privation theory of evil, that evils are lacks of proper
goods, and that only good is fully real, fully existent and self-subsistent.)
The goods cited here include benevolence, fortitude, sympathy, determination, industry, and the like. It is argued that these goods cannot exist in
the absence of certain evils such as pain, suffering of self or others, and
that their goodness is such that it provides a justification of the evils on
which they depend. These goods may not require a great deal of evil, but
that they depend for their existence on the existence of some evil, is
claimed to show that some evil can be justified by reference to these goods,

---

[4] *St. Thomas and the Problem of Evil*, pp. 16-7.

and hence that the traditional problem of evil (Problem 1) is not really a problem for the theist.

A number of replies are possible here. I shall note them briefly here and develop them later when discussing the problem concerning the amount of evil, for they loom larger in discussions of and proposed solutions to that problem.

Firstly, it is not true that benevolence in the sense of good will to others depends on the existence of evil. One can feel and show good will towards a happy, contented, wealthy friend. One can show sympathy and concern if one believes another to be suffering – there need be no real suffering. (Here it might be objected that one could not get the concept of suffering without experience of it by oneself or someone else.) One can show courage in the face of apparent danger – there need be no real danger. More important, the value judgment involved is completely untenable. The goods concerned are not intrinsic goods; and their instrumental value is much less than is assumed in this argument. These facts become evident if we consider the human situation. We do not deem the goodness of the goods as being such as to justify artificially introducing evils into the world. Only a very evil husband would beat, torture, torment his wife, and ultimately kill her in order to develop such goods as fortitude, tolerance, kindness in the wife and compassion, sympathy and benevolence in her friends, parents, children, and neighbours. Such a plea in justification of his gravely evil conduct by the husband would be ludicrous. It is equally ludicrous at the divine level. Similarly, in the human situation, we do not spread disease as a means of increasing such goods. We deem germ warfare to be a gravely evil form of warfare. Yet those who advance this kind of argument to justify the existence of *some* evil, that is, in order to show that the traditional problem of evil (Problem 1) is a pseudo-problem, are suggesting that God deliberately allowed some evil, be it pain, suffering, disease, in order to allow or even to foster such goods. *This is the real reply to Ahern's argument.*

Many theists, seemingly under the influence of Kant, although in direct opposition to his ethic, and who none the less operate with a utilitarian calculus, for instance N. Smart, make much of the importance of temptation for there to be true virtue and true moral good.[5] Kant himself provided the reply to this view. The Holy Will is not subject to temptation, yet it is wholly good. For the utilitarian, there is no intrinsic value in the activity of resisting temptation *qua* resisting temptation.

It is significant that no major moral philosopher, and no utilitarian of

[5] "Omnipotence, Evil and Supermen", *Philosophy,* XXXVI, 1961.

note apart from Rashdall has been inclined to list the goods noted by theists, among the intrinsic goods; indeed, the absence of the most generally acknowledged intrinsic goods, pleasure, happiness, beauty, knowledge, rationality, self-perfection, from the theists' discussions here is very significant.[6] Further considerations against this kind of solution to the problem created by the actual evils in the world, will be set out in Chapter 8.

The Theists' Argument as resting on an ideal utilitarian ethic and calculus. The foregoing discussion brings out how much the theists' claim turns on the acceptance in part or *in toto* of a certain kind of ethic, and on the rejection of other normative ethical theories. The value judgments implicit in the above arguments are much more obviously to be derived from an ideal utilitarian ethic than from any other normative ethic. An ethical theory such as that of Kant, to the effect that it is never right to perform certain kinds of acts in order to achieve goods, for instance, that it is never right to treat persons simply as means, would involve a rejection of such judgments. Knowingly to allow harm to one or some to occur, that good may come to others, is permissible on a utilitarian calculus. It is not morally permissible in terms of many other ethical theories. Relevant here is the fact that the proposed solution relates to some/any evil – the kind or amount is not specified.

Upto this point, it is the theists' argument from examples of goods providing justifications for evils which has been examined. The theist also argues that those seeking to show that the traditional problem of evil (Problem 1) is even a *prima facie* one need to set out an analytic ethical principle which brings out the incompatibility between the existence of evil and the perfections of God. Typically, those who take the problem of evil seriously refer to the kind or amount of evil, for example, they refer to the existence of excessive, unnecessary, or unjustified evil. Problem 1 is a problem concerning the compatibility of any evil with an all-perfect creator.

It might be thought that the critic could argue that a world wholly free of evil is better than one with evil in it, and that a wholly good, all-powerful being would always create the better rather than the less good world. I suggest that the latter is true. However, in reply to the former part of the assertion, the theist may and does argue by reference to organic unities, or complexes, that a whole or a complex containing evil may be more valuable than one that is wholly good.

---

[6] Although G. E. Moore did not note such moral goods as intrinsic goods, he argued that moral evils such as lasciviousness and cruelty are intrinsic evils. See *Principia Ethica*, pp. 209 ff.

The latter argument appears to be in principle sound. Yet, in principle, it allows that a whole containing the evil of the brutal, sadistic murder of an innocent child, the kinds of evils described in Chapter 2, may be an organic whole, or a complex, more valuable than a good which is good through and through. Further, if this argument is to serve the theists' end, this complex must be better than any complex composed solely of goods. I suggest that an all-powerful, wholly good creator could create or would create a world which is wholly free of such evils, and which is better than any such world. It is true that it is impossible here for the writer to formulate an analytic connecting link. It is not therefore true that an analytic ethical connecting link does not exist. Neither is it true that there cannot be set out a synthetic necessary ethical principle which brings out the incompatibility between the perfections of God and the existence of any evil.

CHAPTER VII

THE BEST OF ALL POSSIBLE WORLDS

It has been argued that an all-perfect creator must create the best possible world, and that he did precisely this in creating this world. Leibniz's name is that most commonly associated with this view, Leibniz commonly being interpreted as offering as solutions both to the traditional problem of evil concerning the existence of any evil, and to the problem concerning the actual evil which occurs, the contention that this is the best of all possible worlds, and hence that God has done all that he could do. Evil, and the actual evil to be found in the world, therefore constitute no problem according to Leibniz.

As against this interpretation of Leibniz, I suggest that Leibniz simply sought to bring out what is implied by the thesis that God exists. The problem of evil is that concerning whether, given the fact of evil, God exists. Leibniz accepts as datum that God exists. This is not up for question for him in this context. From this starting point, he argues that this must be the best of all possible worlds, for a perfect being would and could only create the best of all possible worlds. It is then argued that the evil which occurs is justified as being an unavoidable element in the best of all possible worlds. Thus we find Leibniz arguing:

"Now this supreme wisdom, united to a goodness that is no less infinite, cannot but have chosen the best. For as a lesser evil is a kind of good, even so a lesser good is a kind of evil if it stands in the way of a greater good; and there would be something to correct in the actions of God if it were possible to do better. As in mathematics, when there is no maximum nor minimum, in short nothing distinguished, everything is done equally, or when that is not possible nothing at all is done: so it may be said likewise in respect of perfect wisdom, which is no less orderly than mathematics, that if there were not the best (optimum) among all possible worlds, God would not have produced any." [1]

[1] *Theodicy,* London, Routledge & Kegan Paul, 1952, translated by E. M. Huggard.

And:

"Thus, if the smallest evil that comes to pass in the world were missing in it, it would no longer be this world; which, with nothing omitted and all allowance made, was found the best by the Creator who chose it." [2]

And:

"To be the best, and to be desired by those who are most virtuous and wise, comes to the same thing. And it may be said that, if we could understand the structure and the economy of the universe, we should find that it is made and directed as the wisest and most virtuous could wish it, since God cannot fail to do thus." [3]

The argument then runs: God exists. Being all-perfect, he must create the best possible world, for there would be an imperfection in God if he chose to create a less good world when a better world is possible. There must be a best possible world, for otherwise it would always be possible for God to have created a better world, *ad infinitum,* in which case he would not have created any world at all. That he created this world shows therefore both that there is such a thing as a best possible world, and that this is it. Leibniz anticipated the reply that a better world than this can be imagined and hence is possible, arguing in Paragraph 9 from the interconnectedness of universes, and in 10 by an appeal to God's perfection, thus:

"It is true that one may imagine possible worlds without sin and without unhappiness, and one could make some like Utopian or Sevarambian romances: but these same worlds again would be very inferior to ours in goodness. I cannot show you this in detail. For can I know and can I present infinities to you and compare them together? But you must judge with me *ab effectu,* since God has chosen this world as it is. We know, moreover, that often an evil brings forth a good whereto one would not have attained without that evil. Often indeed two evils have made one great good." [4]

Leibniz goes on to note that although St. Paul disapproved of doing evil that good may come, that we none the less cannot disapprove of God doing this. He cites the cases where "evils", for example, bitterness of taste, may lead to greater good in the form of pleasure. He stresses the amount of good, and questions the view that there is a vast amount of evil and little good by pointing to the wonderful way in which the fragile machines,

Essays on the Justice of God and the Freedom of Man in the Origin of Evil, Para. 8, page 128.

[2] *Ibid.,* Para. 9, pp. 128-9.
[3] *Ibid.,* Para. 201, p. 252.
[4] *Ibid.,* Para. 10, p. 129.

human and animal organisms maintain themselves, fragile and corruptible though they be. He also deplores the attention given to human misery as simply increasing it. This mode of reasoning gives rise to the feeling of many readers of Leibniz's *Theodicy* that Leibniz had no real grasp of the enormity of human suffering. It is philosophers such as Leibniz who make it so important and necessary to enter into the kind of discussion into which I entered in Chapter 2 of this work. It is vital for a full and comprehensive treatment of the problems which arise from the existence of evil that the world be seen as it is and not in a romanticised way.

Leibniz's "solution" to the problem of evil, if it may be called that, is more important than this brief discussion may suggest, and this, because a great many of the favoured proposed solutions to the problem of evil implicitly assume that this world is the best of all possible worlds. An attempt will be made in the next Chapter to illustrate this.

In assessing Leibniz's account ethical and metaphysical criticisms need to be considered. Two distinct ethical questions need to be asked: (i) Suppose it be conceded that this is the best of all possible worlds, it may still be asked whether this fact alone would show that God was justified in creating the world. Is the only feature of the world that is relevant to the justification of evil, that this is the best possible world? (ii) Is Leibniz right in claiming that any world short of the best world would not do, that evil would be lacking in justification in a world which was not the best possible world?

(i) I suggest that the nature and content of the world are relevant to the problem of evil, and this, independently of whether this is the best possible world. This becomes evident by considering what may indeed be the case, that this world is one in which there is more evil than good. In such a world, the evil would lack a justification, whether or not the world was the best possible world. A wholly good, omnipotent God would refrain from creating a world in which evil predominated even were this the best possible world he could create. I suggest therefore that the underlying suggestion that evil is justified if this is the best of all possible worlds is mistaken; the kinds and amounts of goods and evils are also relevant to the problems distinguished in Chapter 1.

(ii) Equally, it can be questioned whether or not God is obliged as a wholly perfect being to create the better rather than the less good world, the best rather than the better, if there is such a thing as the best possible world. Many theists argue that God is obliged simply to make a good world, but not necessarily the better or the best. They use as their model the human situation. If a man does good but could have done better we rarely feel justified in blaming him for not doing better. The concept of a supererogatory act arises out of this belief that the better act is usually not strictly obligatory. Whatever we may wish to say about so-called supererogatory acts – the concept and its applications are open to debate – I suggest that in the human situation we take note of human limitations and weakness, the fact that human persons have to exert themselves, forgo goods, make sacrifices, and the like. It is for these reasons that we normally accept a good act rather than demanding the better or the best possible act open to another person. None the less we believe that people need to have good reasons for refraining from bringing into being significant goods, or for not eliminating great evils where this can be done without effort or inconvenience. In the case of God the 'exculpating' circumstances and factors cannot hold. He knows what he can successfully achieve, and he does not need to exert any effort of will, make sacrifices, or the like, as human persons may, in order to achieve his ends. Thus the human parallel does not apply. An all-perfect God as such must prefer the better to the good, and the best if there is such a thing, to the better.

A consequential question following on from this concerns whether, if an all-perfect God must create the better (or best if there is one) world, he can be said to be free and omnipotent. Leibniz's God, it would seem, would have no real choice between the creation of alternative worlds if he can opt only for the one world (or for one from the many equally best possible worlds if there be such, which Leibniz would seem to deny). This again is a special instance of the more general problem of omnipotence and perfection, of power and goodness.

The more basic challenge to Leibniz's account takes the form of denying that the concept of the best of all possible worlds is a coherent one. Thomists such as Journet argue that the concept is incoherent, meaningless, without application. Journet writes:

"The notion of the best of all possible worlds is by definition unrealizable – like that of the fastest possible speed – for 'whatever thing he has made, God could make a better one', and so on indefinitely. To demand that God, to be above reproach, must make the best of all possible worlds is to demand him to make what is not feasible, and to give existence to something absurd." [5]

The basis of this objection is the aspect of infinity in the range of worlds it is possible for God to create. Once one specifies the features of the best world, a better world can be conceived of as possible. J. Hick rejects this

[5] *Op. cit.,* pp. 117-8.

contention but seemingly only because he fails to understand it.[6] He argues that once the criterion of excellence is stated a world may be judged to be the best of possible worlds. This is to miss the point of Journet's contention. His contention is that it is the criterion of the best of all possible worlds which does not admit of being set out, for in respect of any criterion it is always possible to imagine or indicate another criterion such that a world conforming with it would surpass in goodness a world conforming with the former criterion. The kinds of models which may be used to illustrate Journet's contention are concepts such as 'the largest water-melon possible' – compare with 'the largest water-melon in Africa'; 'the best possible painting' – compare with 'the best existing painting'; 'the biggest possible universe', and so on. I suggest that Journet is right in rejecting as incoherent, the concept of the best possible world.

Two important implications follow from this. The more important for our purposes is that the acceptance of Journet's contention in no way invalidates the basic ethical principle underlying Leibniz's argument which was discussed under (ii) above, namely that an all-perfect being ought/must always to choose the better rather than the less good, unless he has some morally adequate reason for not doing so. As noted above the notion of a morally adequate reason of the kind that would be relevant here has no application to God. The second implication would seem to be that the same moves can be made in respect of God not having created a better world than this one, *ad infinitum*. This raises further difficulties concerning the concept of omnipotence.

---

[6] *Op. cit.*, pp. 167-8.

CHAPTER VIII

THE WORLD AS GOOD OVER-ALL

If the theists' arguments discussed in Chapter 6 to the effect that some evil is compatible with the perfection of the creator of this world since some evil may be justified by reference to good were successful, the problem of evil would become the remaining problems noted in Chapter 1, with the main interest of theists and their critics centering on Problem 2 concerning the actual evil that occurs. In spite of the fact that it is the first form of the traditional problem of evil that is most commonly alluded to as "the problem of evil", it is this second problem which is most commonly discussed and towards which most of the famous proposed solutions have been directed. For this reason, whilst some of this Chapter will relate to the possibility of a solution to the first problem, the bulk of the discussion will be concerned with an examination of solutions which have been advanced to the second problem concerning the actual kinds and amounts of evil which are to be found in the world.

It is extremely difficult to organize and systematically treat of the vast range of proposed solutions which proceed by seeking to show that although there is great evil in the world, it is justified because the world is good over-all. To help deal with them in less than a random way, I shall make use of the inaptly named distinction between physical evil – pain, suffering, natural ugliness – and moral evil. Some of the proposed solutions relate only to one of these two kinds of evil, and then to certain types within the one kind. Other proposed solutions, like that examined in the previous Chapter, relate to both kinds and all sub-kinds of evil, for example to animal pain, pain and suffering in young, innocent children, pain and suffering in adults due to natural causes, or to accidents by other human beings, that is, unavoidable errors of judgment, and to deliberate, morally evil acts.

Any proposed solution relating to the actual kinds and amounts of evil which occur would, if successful, *ipso facto,* be a solution to the first

traditional problem of evil. In showing that a proposed solution is unsuccessful in dealing with evil as we know it, it is not being claimed that it
may not be restated or offered as a solution to Problem 1. This Chapter
will therefore be a supplement to Chapter 6 in the sense that brief assess-
ments of solutions advanced in answer to the problem posed by actual
evil are also or alternatively solutions to the problem posed by any/some
evil.

The accounts which will be considered here are: In respect of *physical
evil*: (i) There can be no pleasure if no pain; and more generally, that physical goods are impossible without physical evils. (ii) Physical evil in the
form of pain is justified as a warning system. (iii) Physical evil is God's
warning to men. This is commonly associated with a doctrine of the atonement. (iv) Physical evil is God's punishment of man. In its more refined
forms, this line of argument appeals to original sin. (v) Physical evil is
explained as being an unavoidable result of the operation of generally
beneficial laws of nature; if there is to be a law-governed universe, there
must be collisions and hence calamities. Some such as Hick specially stress
the role of evolutionary development in producing man, and complete
their accounts by reference to theological doctrines which involve reference
to goods to be enjoyed by some or by all mankind. (vi) There is also the
partial treatment of the existence of evil by St. Thomas and his followers
including J. Maritain, in terms of a world of various orders being better
than one with fewer orders, where the plurality of orders involves there being corruptible and peccable beings, some of whom will be corrupted or/
and fail. (vii) It is argued that the universe is better for there being physical
evil in it, as it leads to the higher moral goods. Two versions of this
argument, an aesthetic and a moral version, will be examined. (viii) It
is argued, as by C. A. Campbell, that immortality is relevant to the explanation and justification of evil in that it provides an opportunity for
correcting the injustices which occur in this world. (ix) Faith is claimed to
provide, not a solution, but grounds for believing that there is a solution.
(x) Finally there are Ahern's and Plantinga's arguments that we cannot
know that there is not a solution, hence we cannot know that a solution
is logically impossible.

With *moral evil* the accounts to be considered here are: (i) Free will
alone provides a justification of moral evil. (ii) Moral evil as justified by
the goods freedom makes to be possible. (iii) Moral evil as justified by
both free will itself and the goods it makes to be possible. The goods mentioned in solutions of types (ii) and (iii) vary from writer to writer, ranging
from goods such as fortitude, sympathy, compassion, benevolence and the

like, to a triumph in the face of adversity, and/or soul-making and the enterprise of a loving union with God.

Obviously these are neither the totality of types nor ranges of proposed solutions, but they do include the more important and more celebrated ones.

SECTION A – SOLUTIONS TO THE PROBLEM POSED BY PHYSICAL EVIL

(i) There can be no pleasure if no pain:
physical goods are impossible without physical evils

A rather desperate attempt to solve the problem of physical evil consists in the contention that in a real sense pain is an essential background experience for the experiencing or enjoying pleasure. Two different claims occur here. The one is that pleasure in some way involves the elimination of a pain. Here the craving of a desire is pointed to as being essential to the pleasure that follows upon the satisfying of the craving. Against this is the fact that there are many pleasures which do not involve a prior craving. The pleasures of sight and taste are such. The pleasure of looking at things, at beautiful works of art, a beautiful scene, an oceanscape, a patch of colour, a beautiful horse, and the like, are pleasures which come upon us without prior craving. So too when we experience a new pleasant taste, or the scent of a rose, or the touch of velvet, we experience it as pleasant without there having been any prior craving. We can develop cravings for these pleasures but the pleasure itself is not dependent on there being a craving. The sight, taste, smell, the pleasing touch can take us entirely by surprise. The pleasures of the intellect are also of this kind, although with some individuals the pleasures of curiosity may involve a craving before the pleasure, this is not typical of early enjoyments of pleasures of the intellect. Cravings may come to develop but this is generally a later development not a precursor of all intellectual pleasure.

The second form that this general claim that pleasure involves the existence of some pain takes, is that it is necessary to know opposites to know either, hence we must experience and know pain to experience and know that we are experiencing pleasure. In spite of its popularity this argument is mistaken. If we could not know pleasure until we knew pain, and *vice versa,* we could come to know neither. We come to experience and to know the one and then to contrast it with the other. There must be an initial experience of the one or the other. Further, it is evident that a person could go through life without ever experiencing any pleasure and yet suffer deeply from pains such as toothaches, broken bones, and the like. Superior beings such as angels must surely be capable of experiencing pleasure, albeit higher pleasures, yet they need never experience pain or suffering. Further, even were knowledge of pain essential for the experience of pleasure, very much less than occurs would provide the required knowledge. One toothache would be sufficient for us to know what pain is. This means at the least much less pain is necessary for us to have a capacity to enjoy pleasure, and that if the main arguments above are sound, no pain is essential as a precondition for enjoying pleasure.

The contention that physical goods are impossible without physical evils, would seemingly amount to the contention that goods such as happiness, pleasure, and those goods upon which these depend such as health, are impossible without physical evils such as pain and suffering. (I myself include among intrinsic goods, goods such as knowledge, beauty, aesthetic excellence, rationality, and self-perfection). Health, by definition, presupposes the absence of disease; and it is possible without pain and suffering. If it is argued that health relates to a corruptible being, which of its nature is corruptible, and hence that health depends on the possibility of ill-health and in some cases on actual ill-health, since among corruptibles some will be corrupted, this reduces to the Thomist argument already considered and which will briefly be considered again in this Section. The basic objection is to the claim about the necessity of the ill-health if there are to be healthy individuals. So too there seems no reason why it should be supposed that happiness involves the existence or even reference to suffering or pain. A more common argument is that higher goods depend for their existence on the existence of pain and suffering. This is a distinct claim and will be discussed later in this Chapter. The other goods I wish to claim to be intrinsic goods are even more obviously independent of the existence of evils. Rationality, knowledge, beauty, and the like, do not presuppose for their existence, the existence of corresponding evils.

This whole line of argument relates to seeking to justify the existence of some evil, but not all the evil which actually occurs. Even if this kind of account had any basis in fact, it would not relate to all physical evil. Many wish to allow that animals may experience pain and even suffering; fewer might be prepared to argue as strongly that animals experience pleasure, and even less, happiness.

(ii) Physical evil in the form of pain as justified as a useful, even necessary warning system

The argument here is that pain has a real justification as being a means of warning us of the possibility of evils, of self-injuries and self-neglect, of the dangers of diseases and the danger of death. If hunger did not cause discomfort, and even pain, we may not eat; if heat did not burn and hurt, we may unknowingly severely burn ourselves, doing permanent, irreparable harm; if our teeth did not ache when they decayed, we may not seek treatment with greater evils resulting; if ulcers did not cause discomfort, their presence would not be known and death would follow; if malignant tumours did not cause pain, their existence may be ignored, and so on. The various warning systems which we have in the form of traffic lights to increase safety on the roads, the use of warning labels on bottles of poisons, the evidence of X-ray examinations and other tests, are in some measure at least parasitic on the pain warning system. They are heeded at least in part because we do not wish to be hurt; we do not want to suffer pain. Pain therefore does seem to have one real use and to be at least in part justified by virtue of its usefulness. Is this really so?

The first ground for doubting this kind of justification is to be found by considering that of which pain is a warning. It is a warning either of further pain or of suffering (i.e. of more intense pain or suffering), or it is a warning of the danger or imminence of death, often of a painful death. In so far as pain is simply a warning of further pain, or in so far as it is a warning of suffering, to that extent its feature of being a warning system does nothing towards showing it to be justified. Such a line of justification would amount to claiming that it is justified as being a warning of itself or of something very like itself, namely suffering. In so far as pain is a warning of death, its justification is equally strange. If one's life were wholly pleasant and happy, it would seem that pain introduced as a warning of death would lack a justification. If one knew that one had seventy years of happy life to live, pain on the way would not make up for itself. Compare here being on a very enjoyable holiday and having painful reminders that one had only a fortnight, a week, a day, to go. I suggest that life, even more evidently than the holiday, would be better for not having the painful warnings. Further, if death is regarded as the termination of all existence, it is difficult to see any evil in an enjoyable life being terminated without pain or suffering to the person, unless others are harmed and/or a good being could have prolonged it, and if passing on to another existence were not possible and equally full of opportunities for higher level activities. In brief, pain as a warning system usually warns of more pain, and at the same time usually creates suffering in the form of fear, anxiety, worry, concern, regret in others.

A second ground for questioning this account relates to the issue of whether pain is always or even essentially a warning device. Here I wish to suggest that it is by no means always such. That pain is not necessarily a warning of ill-health is evident from the fact of labour pains. So too, neurotic pains of individuals who have no control over these pains seem to have no evident justification as warning signs – of what are they a warning? Further, there are the pains of animals who suffer most of the diseases of human beings – degeneration from old age, brain tumours, arthritis, cancer, and the like, where their suffering has little or no value as part of a warning mechanism. The warning simply makes their condition worse. If they suffered no pain whilst suffering from such diseases they could be much better off. This leads to the suggestion that the pain which is a warning of avoidable pain, suffering, or death, and which helps in its further prevention or lessening, must be claimed to justify that pain which does not have this fortunate result. The kind of account to be offered here would be that one has to take and judge the system as a whole, and that it is a more satisfactory warning system than any other. But again the doubt arises because so much of its successful warning is simply against future pain.

A third ground for questioning the justification of pain as a warning system springs from the possibility that there are or may be warning systems which involve less evil and/or yet be more efficient. Clearly the claim that the pain warning system as we know it is the only possible type of warning system available to an all-powerful, all-wise God is untenable. Even we human beings can imagine a vast range of alternative systems, for instance, an auditory one, one in terms of vibrations, or one in terms of colour changes. Some of these we already have and use. Any claim that this is *the only possible warning system* available to an all-perfect, all-wise God would in effect involve the admission that God really is a finite being. Relevant here is Hume's contention that an alternative arrangement in terms of diminution of pleasure would be possible and preferable.[1] The claim that this is *the best and most efficient type of warning system* is also open to challenge. Since the pain warning system involves the evils of pain and suffering, actual and anticipated, and since it is an inefficient

---

[1] See *Dialogues Concerning Natural Religion*, Pt. XI and also J. Hick, *Evil and the God of Love*, pp. 338-343.

system as will now be argued in more detail, it is unlikely to be the best possible system.

It has already been noted that pain is not always a warning of disorder, and that where it is, as with much animal pain due to injury and disease, it is a useless warning which worsens the total situation. Further, where it is a warning, the severity of the pain is often not related to the seriousness of the disorder or disease. In an efficient system, and certainly in the best possible system, there would not be injuries and diseases without warning signs, and the urgency of the warning would be related or proportional to the seriousness of the danger. Pain is not a reliable, efficient warning system for many diseases, for example, tuberculosis, cancer, venereal disease, to mention only three major diseases. Here we resort to other devices, using instead of pain reports, cough reports, X-rays, feeling for lumps, blood tests, and the like. If, in such matters, we confined our reliance on warning symptoms to pain warnings, the diseases would often advance to incurable states before being detected. Another type of case which tells against the efficiency of the pain warning system is that of injuries which at first are experienced as not unpleasant, and even as pleasant, for instance, injuries due to frostbite, those incurred under the influence of or as caused by drugs. Another objection relates to or involves the distinction between the sensation of pain in the nervous system and the felt experience of pain. Hick and others point out that one may suffer pain, that is be injured, and feel no distress, but sometimes even pleasure.[2] They cite the footballer, the soldier, and the like, who suffer injuries, and the person who has a frontal leucotomy operation. In such cases the pain warning system is inefficient.

In brief, for a warning system involving an evil such as pain, and the invariable resultant evils of suffering of various kinds, to have a claim to be considered to be justified, it would need to fulfil at least the following conditions. It would have to be such that no other equally efficient/inefficient system involving less or no pain was possible, and that no other kind of system be more efficient. An efficient pain system, unlike the one we know, would have to be universally distributed to all sentient beings. It must be invariably reliable, giving a warning always when a warning was required, and only when required, namely when there was a disorder or a danger of a disorder, and in such a way that the warning gave some indication of the seriousness of the disorder.

Suffering. Pain, localized felt pain, constitutes only part of the problem of physical evil. Another important element in physical evil, and the

[2] *Op. cit.,* ch. XV.

one that is commonly regarded as more serious than pain, is suffering. Consider the suffering, indeed misery, that comes from a sense of despair, of hopelessness, worry, anxiety about the future, fear, melancholy – the healthy and the neurotic conditions – the distress caused by the sense of despair, futility, worthlessness, grief, loneliness, where these may be such as to drive a person to take his life. These forms of suffering are real, and it is probable that more persons commit suicide from these forms of suffering than from pain itself. It is possible today to do much to lessen pain; it is more difficult to alleviate and eliminate suffering. Suffering is not part of a warning mechanism and it need in no way be related to human defects or disorders in the sufferer. Much suffering is natural in the sense of being a product of highly valued traits, such as sensitivity, humility, affection, and concern for others. It is therefore important to stress that whatever may be the case for justifying pain as a warning system that line of argument leaves untouched a major area of the problem of physical evil. It contributes not at all towards providing an explanation and justification of a major aspect of the problem, and is unsuccessful with that aspect towards which it is directed.

(iii) Physical evil as God's warning to men

This is a line of argument which has been seriously advanced by theists, and one which in its simplest form has impressed ordinary believers, the more so the more ignorant they have been. G. H. Joyce here observes of natural disasters:

"The earthquake and the volcano serve a moral end which more than compensates for the physical evil which they cause. The awful nature of these phenomena, the overwhelming power of the forces at work, and man's utter helplessness before them, rouse him from the religious indifference to which he is so prone. They inspire a reverential awe of the Creator who made them and controls them, and a salutary fear of violating the laws which He has imposed." [3]

It is in this context that the Christian beliefs concerning the atonement and personal immortality are often alluded to as justifying such evil. God warns sinners of his power, and thereby through the atoning sacrifice of Jesus, believers are able to come to a loving relationship with God. Without such a reference to an immortal existence in which occurs the good of men freely responding to God's love, this account fails to offer a justification of these natural calamities. What after all is of value in a res-

[3] *Op. cit.*, p. 596.

ponse through fear and power-worship to the destructive acts of power? Such a response must be regarded as unfortunate rather than be lauded as a good. It is strange that Joyce, whose whole discussion shows sensitive awareness that reverence for mere power is very different from reverence and awe for a wholly perfect God, should invoke such an argument. There are other objections to this attempt to justify natural evils. In so far as it is dependent on reference to the Christian doctrine of the atonement, to that extent it is involved in the difficulties encountered by that doctrine. As I have argued elsewhere, the various different doctrines of the atonement involve a denial of God's wisdom, his power, and/or his goodness, and themselves proceed on the basis of untenable moral beliefs.[4] Further, the basic claim made in the argument, that such calamities serve the moral purpose of inspiring a reverential awe of God, is generally false. On the contrary they arouse in many doubts and even disbelief in God's goodness and even in his existence. If God's intention was to have the effect indicated by Joyce, then his claims to be both omnipotent and omniscient would have to be challenged. More basically, the use of physical evil to achieve this object, is hardly the course one would expect a benevolent God to adopt when other, more effective, less evil methods are available to him, for example, those by way of beneficial miracles, special revelation, and the like.

(iv) Physical evil as God's punishment for sin

As noted in my article "God and Evil", this kind of explanation was advanced to explain the Lisbon earthquake in which 40,000 people were killed.[5] Voltaire rightly replied to the argument asking: "Did God in this earthquake select the 40,000 least virtuous of the Portugese citizens?" The distribution of disease, pain, and suffering in this world is in no obvious way related to the virtue of the persons afflicted, and popular saying ("The devil looks after his own") has it that the distribution is slanted in the opposite direction. The only way of meeting this fact is to suggest that all human beings including young children who are deformed even before birth are such miserable sinners that our offences are of such enormity that God would be justified in punishing all of us as severely as it is possible for human beings to be punished. Even then God's apparent caprice in the selection of those he punishes would require explanation and justification.

---

[4] "Why the Cross?", *The Rationalist Annual*, 1965.
[5] *Philosophical Quarterly*, 10, 1960. I draw heavily on this article in this Chapter.

Clearly young children who suffer greatly, and who are so constituted that they will do so before birth – born with hydrocephalus, deaf, dumb, and blind, or with deformed limbs – cannot plausibly be claimed to suffer because of their sins. To try to appeal in a crude way to original sin here would simply be to attribute another form of injustice to God.

None the less we do find theists, for example, C. Journet following Aquinas, appealing to original sin as part of his explanation of suffering. His is a more refined theory of original sin and of how it relates to man's suffering than some other such theories, yet it too must be rejected for substantially the above reasons. Journet, after observing that:

"All the trials in our human lives are due to sin, though not all in the same way: some are attributable to original sin, others to our personal sins." [6]

He then goes on to explain that:

"St. Thomas writes that at baptism Christ immediately delivers man 'from everything which affects his person, i.e. the guilt of original sin and the pain which follows from it, the privation of the divine vision. But the penalties of the present life, such as death, hunger, thirst, etc., affect *human nature* from which they flow as from their source since it was stripped of original justice; and that is why these miseries, *defectus*, will only disappear at the time of the ultimate repairing of our nature by the glorious resurrection.' " [7]

It is important to note that these accounts relate only to human pain and suffering, and not to that to which animals are exposed. This means that those who accept such a line of justification of human suffering – as in thirst, hunger, death – are committed to the unlikely view that the pains of thirst, starvation, death in animals have a radically different justification. This is freely acknowledged. Some adopt the account implicit in (v), others that in (vi) below, and others offer other accounts again, most stressing the vast difference between animal pain and human pain and suffering, and the little knowledge we have of the former.

(v) Physical evil as an unavoidable result of the operation of generally beneficial laws of nature

C. A. Campbell sets out this argument in *Selfhood and Godhood*.[8] Its essence is that the world is a good world, that it is better for having the na-

---

[6] *Op. cit.*, p. 218.
[7] *Ibid.*, p. 220. Reference to *Summa Theologiae*, III, 69, 3, ad. 3.
[8] Pp. 298 ff.

tural laws it has than it would be without any laws, that any law-governed universe would have to contain some evil. (Corporeal bodies must sometimes collide, etc.). The kind of point being made here is that if there are laws such as the law of gravity we are able to plan and order our lives on the basis of certain definite expectations, and many goods will accordingly be possible but the price we pay is in terms of landslides, earthquakes, collisions, and other effects of gravity. Campbell offers this solution tentatively and with reservations, yet he finally seems to accept it as being an adequate solution when it is supplemented by reference to an immortal existence in which the injustices in this life are compensated for in the next life. His expressed doubts and reservations concern whether the special kind of undeserved suffering is an inevitable incident, and whether bodies incapable of intense and prolonged agony are possible, and thirdly, whether the price paid in suffering may not be too high a price to pay for having a world at all.

There are a number of difficulties in the way of this argument. Thus, even if it were conceded that the laws are useful, and indeed the best possible laws, and this I shall question later, it is clear that there would have been vastly less evil in the world if man had been able *to know* these laws sooner and more easily. Even now there are many laws of nature relating to diseases which are not known to man. Knowledge of the laws of nature has enabled man to make better use of things in the world, to act without causing or enduring suffering which otherwise would have been unavoidable, and to prevent great suffering by eradicating evils such as diseases. Consider here what a knowledge of the laws of nature has made to be possible in terms of goods produced; consider also the vast evils which have been eliminated or now prevented or lessened by the use of this knowledge. Malaria was very widespread and was a great killer, but now because of our comparatively recently acquired knowledge of it, it is much less widespread and much less often a killer. This is true to a greater or less extent of most other killer diseases – bubonic plague, tuberculosis, poliomyelitis, cholera, typhoid, meningitis, to mention only a few such diseases. It is our ignorance of the causes of diseases (that is of the laws relating to them) such as arthritis, cancer, and many other diseases which now bring suffering and whose symptoms can be treated or their progress retarded, but often no cure effected, which allows this state of affairs to prevail. Consider also how much suffering could have been avoided if penicillin had been discovered 2000 years ago, or if all that is now known about viruses, microbes, and other disease organisms, and about carriers of diseases, mosquitoes, fleas, ticks, flies, and the like, had been known two millenia ago.

A law-governed universe in which all the laws were known such that we could organize our lives effectively on the basis of them would be one thing; our law-governed universe, being one in which we do not yet know what all the laws are, is another. It is because of our limited reason, our grave defects as human beings of limited intelligence, limited memory, limited powers generally, that many of the nastier evils in the world continue when, had we knowledge and intelligence of a higher order, we could make use of the law-governed behaviour of things to reduce the evilness of the effects of the operation of the laws. It is not clear that creation of a species with more adequate intellectual powers is beyond the scope of the competence of an omnipotent being. A reply here that man himself is a product of the operation of these very same laws, *via* the evolutionary process, will not do, as God is claimed to be both omniscient and omnipotent. He could foresee man's emergence and could therefore have planned a world with better equipped sentient beings emerging. Of all the combinations of law-governed universes with emergent 'men' that are possible for God, it seems very improbable, when full account is taken of the nature, complexity, and obscurity of the laws of nature of this world on the one hand, and of the limitations of the human intellect on the other, that an all-perfect being could not create a better world, and one with less evil in it, than this world. The point here relates to the amount of evil, that there would have been less evil if God had given the average man the mental powers of a Newton or an Einstein, and they proportionately greater mental powers again. Reference to evolutionary development does not invalidate this claim. No doubt some cynical theists will observe here that the knowledge gained by Newton, Einstein, and other great scientists has been used by men to devise destructive weapons, and to bring about abominable evils. This is true although it is not true that overall the fruits of scientific discovery are more evil than good. Certainly those who, like Campbell, invoke the argument from the value of laws of nature and of a knowledge of them, must contend that overall the laws and our knowledge of them bring overall beneficial results.

A second line of objection to this solution relates to the status of the laws of nature. There is a tendency for theists to speak of them as if they were analytic truths, like the laws of logic. (This, as we shall see, is Maritain's view). They are not that. According to Hume and to most in the empiricist tradition, they are simply laws of regularity such that there is and can be no guarantee that the observed regularities will continue for ever. If this is all that the laws of nature are, the suggestion that these laws govern, control, determine, what happens in the world is misleading. Clearly, in terms of the Humean view, there are regularities where we find them. Some regularities are more confidently counted on to continue in the future than are others, although the reality of the problem of induction gives pause for thought as to why this is so. Whether regularities, that is, law-like behaviour occurs everywhere, is a matter for investigation and not a premise that can simply be assumed. For God to intervene to modify a regularity, is obviously very different from his intervening to go against the operation of an inflexible law. There are philosophers, including the present writer, who wish to reject the Humean and other empiricist ac-counts in favour of the view that causal laws are necessary laws, that there are (synthetic) necessary connexions in nature. This is a view, the defence of which presents difficulties no less than those facing the ex-ponent of the empiricist account. However, if much is to be made of the insistence on the value of a law-governed universe, grounds are needed for believing that the law-like nature of the universe will, indeed must, continue indefinitely. We cannot have such grounds on the basis of an empiricist view of causality. Yet the view that these laws are necessary laws either implies a limitation in respect of God's power – this I think to be the case in respect of synthetic necessary laws – or it remains true that God could modify or change the laws when evil could thereby be prevented or reduced.

The theist, in effect, is also involved (and involved in part for the above reasons) in the desperate, and if our discussion in Chapter 7 is sound, in the untenable claim that our law-governed world is the best possible, law-governed world, and that this is indeed the best of all possible worlds. N. Smart suggests this in his "Omnipotence, Evil and Supermen" (an ar-ticle in which he uncritically and insensitively dismisses in one line the possibility that God may be limited by synthetic necessities – no doubt for purposes of *ad hominem argument*).[9] And many others have argued along similar lines. The critic of this solution is challenged to think through the implications of his criticisms. He is told that superficially it seems possible to think of a better, law-governed world, but that this is only because the details are not filled in. This is exactly Leibniz's claim. Or, as with Plantinga, it is observed, by implication, that it has not been shown that a better world is possible, that there is no contradiction involv-

[9] *Philosophy*, XXXVI, 1961, pp. 188-195. Smart here is concerned with Mackie's and Flew's discussions of moral evil, not with solutions to the problem of physical evil. None the less his argument, if sound, commits him to this and the positions discussed below. Thus, in opposing those who stress the inadequacy of solutions to the problem of moral evil, he exposes himself to these difficulties in the context of physical evil.

ed in asserting that God could make a better world. The reply to such moves is the same as that to Leibniz. We are limited, finite beings. Of course we cannot describe in all its detail a law-governed universe superior to this one. We cannot even describe this universe, the one in which we live in all its detail. It has already been noted how limited our knowledge of it is. We do not know all the laws of nature, nor what their ultimate outcome will be (other than the destruction of this planet, among other such related knowledge), although we have reason to suppose that it may ultimately be very unpleasant for some future human beings and animals. All this is, however, beside the point. We are concerned here with what is possible for an all-perfect being. Even if it were not the case, as it has been claimed to be the case, that the concept of the best possible world is incoherent, it would be the height of presumption to suggest that this is the best of all possible worlds, that God could do no better. Yet this is what is implied in Campbell's and Smart's discussions. The possibility of miracles – allowed to be a real possibility by Campbell at least – of even one miracle which could lessen the evil or increase the good, makes nonsense of this contention. (I suggest that those who stress the need for strict *proof* concerning logical impossibilities, for instance, A. Plantinga, would need here to show that it is logically impossible for God to perform even one miracle which would lessen the overall evil or increase the overall good).

It is generally conceded, as it must be, that an omnipotent God can work miracles. Campbell claims that to reduce suffering *significantly* (why is not even a little reduction of value?) God would need to intervene on such a vast scale that he would upset the uniformity of nature and thereby prevent the goods which derive from our being able to count on the uniformity of nature. There is an easy reply to such an argument, namely that if one single miracle which removes one determinate amount of suffering is possible without thereby upsetting our reliance on the laws of nature, it ought to occur. In fact, a good many miracles are possible without our reliance on the uniformity of nature being disturbed. With many diseases there are unexplained, spontaneous cures yet these do not disturb our reliance on the uniformity of nature, not even when research into the causes of spontaneous cures is unsuccessful. In any case, what is important is *our use of our knowledge* of the laws of nature, and only secondarily, the laws themselves. Until God's miraculous intervention got in the way of our knowing and using our knowledge of the laws, miracles could well abound without mischievous side-effects. For the purpose of this argument the possibility of one additional, beneficial miracle is all that is needed to show that Campbell's proposed solution will not do.

Finally here it may be questioned whether the advantages of a law-governed universe are as great as they are represented as being. If we were omniscient, whether the universe were law-like or not, would not matter as we should then be able to foresee the future. Whether we should also be able to foresee and yet still control what happens in the future in the absence of laws, raises a problem or paradox in respect of omniscience, but not in respect of the notion of control as it relates to a law-governed universe. Further, regularity does not involve simple, obvious repetition, but hard to detect uniformities. Since there seems to be no reason why finite beings cannot be omniscient, and hence why an irregular, non-law-governed universe, or one law-governed only in certain areas might not be better than this world, further argument is needed, and such as not to beg the question as does the appeal to evolutionary development, that a law-governed universe is best.

The *ad hominem* argument, which would rest on a denial of the above, could be developed that such universes may be even more challenging, and present even greater obstacles than the present one, and hence make possible greater triumphs for those of limited knowledge and intelligence who succeed.

(vi) A world including various orders of being is better than one
with fewer orders, where the plurality of orders involves there being
corruptible and peccable beings,
some of whom will be corrupted and/or fail

An important part of the Thomistic account of evil, but only a part, is contained in this claim. For the sake of brevity it will be convenient to consider both the evils of physical corruption and of sin here. J. Maritain explains the point by reference to St. Thomas's writings thus:

" 'Perfection of the universe', St. Thomas continues, 'requires therefore that there be some beings who can fall from goodness; and if there are beings who can fall from goodness, the result will be that such defection will in fact sometimes occur in those beings.' For if it is in the nature of things that an event can happen, this event actually will happen sometimes. 'Now, to fall from good, there is the actual evil. That is why evil is found in things: as well as the existence in them of the process of destruction or corruption, for corruption itself is a certain evil.' " [10]

And:

---

[10] *St. Thomas and the Problem of Evil*, p. 6.

"From the moment that created creatures are naturally peccable, there will be some who will in fact sin." [11]

C. Journet, explaining the same theory, observes:

"Evil is permitted for *greater* good. But what greater good? Primarily, and as regards the evil in nature for that universal good which is more precious than that of which particular creatures are deprived by evil. It is better for the world to move on and species to reproduce themselves than for individuals to go on for ever. Philosophy on its own can go no further." [12]

Two basic issues are raised by this account of physical and moral evil. The one relates to the strange value judgment on which it rests, and the other to the nature and meaning of "will happen" used equivalently with "must happen".

The value judgment is not intuitively evident to me, and indeed, seems intuitively false. I cannot see that a world of purely spiritual beings is evidently inferior to one of corporeal beings and spiritual beings, nor that one containing parasites and carnivors is superior to one without such beings. Implicit in the first claim is the contention that a world containing God alone is inferior to that containing God and all the beings that now exist. Similarly with peccable beings. It seems self-evident to me that a world containing wholly virtuous beings (citizens) is better than one containing some who must fail. This is only too evident in the political sphere. Would that there be a society of wholly good, incorruptible persons!

The theory implies that there is some sort of necessity about the falling away of corruptible beings. In respect of animals, their degeneration and death, this necessity seems not to be explained. However, in respect of the corruption of peccable beings such as men, Maritain explains, as we saw above, the necessity as analytic necessity. Here he argues that:

"God, therefore cannot make any creature who is naturally impeccable, any more than He can make a squared circle; these are not necessities independent of God which are forced upon Him from without . . .; these necessities themselves depend on His very essence as His intelligence sees it, seeing at the same time all those ways in which that very essence can be participated in. To annihilate these necessities one would have to annihilate first the very essence of God, and thus we must admit that God can no more create a being by nature impeccable, than He can cease to exist and to be what He is. It is the same sort of necessity." [13]

This is an obscure statement. Maritain is not obviously saying the

---

[11] *God and the Permission of Evil*, pp. 37-8.
[12] *Op. cit.*, p. 86.
[13] *St. Thomas and the Problem of Evil*, pp. 16-7. See footnote p. 97.

necessity is analytic in the usual sense, yet the parallels he draws are on the one hand with analytic necessity as ordinarily understood – and this parallel seems only too evidently inapt – and on the other with the necessity attributed to God as a necessarily existing being, a sense of necessity understood only by those who assent to a belief in the existence of God as a necessarily existent being. Clearly, unless the necessity is analytic necessity, this account fails in its purpose. Reflection about the claim reveals that it is not analytic necessity.

To complete reference to this line of thought about the problem of evil, some further reference to its application in the context of sin (moral evil) by Maritain is necessary. Maritain develops his version of this argument along the lines that sin, suffering and sorrow are permitted for the:

"Consummation of a work of love which transcends the whole order of the world; they are themselves connected to the manifestation of divine goodness as transcending the very universe of creation and expressing itself in the universe of grace or of the transfiguration of love of created persons become God through participation.

The creature's liability to sin is thus the price paid for the outpouring of creative Goodness, which in order *to give itself personally* to the extent that it transforms into itself something other than itself, and must be *freely loved with friendship's love and communion,* and which to be freely loved with friendship's love and communion must create *free* creatures, and which in order to create them free must create them *fallibly* free. Without fallible freedom there can be no created freedom; without created freedom there can be no love in mutual friendship between God and creature; without love in mutual friendship between God and creature, there can be no supernatural transformation of the creature into God, no entering of the creature into the joy of his Lord. Sin, – evil, – is the price of glory." [14]

This particular aspect of the contention that of corruptible creatures, some (all?) must be corrupted, will be discussed further in Section B of this Chapter. It is sufficient here to note the lack of clear argument concerning the nature of the necessity that fallible creatures (some or all?) must sometimes fail. It is not apparently an analytic necessity.

(vii) The universe is better for there being physical evil in it

In a sense the foregoing are all attempts to provide this general kind of solution. I wish here to examine it in two of its more usual forms. In the one form, the proposed solution makes use of an aesthetic model, whilst in the other, it is a simple, direct, moral argument.

[14] *Ibid.,* p. 19.

(a) The Aesthetic Argument

This is basically a special application of the organic wholes/complexes argument, that what appears evil/ugly in isolation in fact contributes to the greater good/beauty of the whole. An implication of the aesthetic version of this argument is that if evil is justified in this way, we ought never to exert ourselves to eliminate any evil, for we should then be detracting from the aesthetic excellence of the universe. The theist could reply to this only by making the remarkable, implausible claim that all the evil that exists, has this kind of justification only so long as it exists, that God foresees our efforts to reduce evils, and has planned the universe so that those evils we eliminate, are eliminated only when they would no longer have such a justification. This would entail that God also foresees all the evils that men introduce, wars and the like, and that he so designed the world that these evils would enhance its excellence. Such an *ad hominem* reply is adequate, but it need not be our only or even our main line of reply. The more basic reply is that the aesthetic model is inappropriate, that pain and suffering in the world are very different from ugly or discordant elements in a painting or a symphony. A further reply is that aesthetic excellence cannot justify the kinds of evils that call for justification. Here it will no doubt be replied that the argument is one by analogy, and is therefore not to be taken literally. If this is so, and obviously it is so, the argument simply becomes a more colourful way of stating the straightforward moral argument which we may now consider.

(b) The Moral Argument

This argument consists in an attempt to explain evil not so much as a *component* of a good whole, seen out of its context, but rather as a *means* to a greater good, and/or a *condition* for greater goods. G. H. Joyce states one version of this kind of argument in the following way:

"Pain is the great stimulant to action. Man, no less than animals, is impelled to work by the sense of hunger. Experience shews that, were it not for this motive, the majority of men would be content to live in indolent ease. Man must earn his bread in the sweat of his brow. And the duty thus imposed is for most men the school of virtue. It is in fulfilling the obligation of daily toil that they learn to practise justice, diligence, patience, charity to others, obedience to those who are over them. ... And one reason, plainly, why God permits suffering is that man may rise to a height of heroism which would otherwise have been altogether beyond his scope. Nor are these the only benefits which it confers. That sympathy for others which is one of the most precious parts of our experience and one of the most fruitful sources of well-doing has its origin in the fellow-feeling engendered by the endurance of similar trials. Furthermore, were it not for these trials, man would think little enough of a future existence, and of the need of striving after his last end. He would be perfectly content with his existence, and would reck little of any higher good. The considerations here briefly advanced suffice at least to shew how important is the office filled by pain in human life, and with what little reason it is asserted that the existence of so much suffering is irreconcilable with the wisdom of the Creator. They shew, moreover, that, where man is concerned, the explanation of suffering is other than in the case of the lower animals. The sufferings of men are directed primarily to the good of the sufferer himself, while they also afford to others an opportunity for the practice of virtue." [15]

And:

"It may be asked whether the Creator could not have brought man to perfection without the use of suffering. Most certainly He could have conferred upon him a similar degree of virtue without requiring any effort on his part. Yet it is easy to see that there is special value attaching to a conquest of difficulties such as man's actual lot demands, and that in God's eyes this may well be an adequate reason for assigning this life to us in preference to another. . . .

We have laid stress on the value of pain in relation to the next life, because it is in the next life, and not in this, that man must attain his last end. But it scarcely needs to be pointed out that pain is a source of many benefits in this life also. The advance of scientific discovery, the gradual improvement of the organization of the community, the growth of material civilization – all these are due in no small degree to the stimulus afforded by pain." [16]

W. D. Niven in "Good and Evil", *Encyclopaedia of Religion and Ethics,* put his version thus:

"Physical evil has been the goad which has impelled men to most of those achievements which made the history of man so wonderful. Hardship is a stern but fecund parent of invention. Where life is easy because physical ills are at a minimum we find man degenerating in body, mind and character." [17]

[15] *Op. cit.,* pp. 594-5.
[16] *Ibid.,* pp. 596-7.
[17] Ed. James Hastings, New York, Charles Scribner's Sons, 1927, VI, p. 325.

J. L. Mackie, in discussing this kind of solution, distinguishes two sorts of solutions, the one being to the effect that evil causes good, and the other that evil is logically necessary for the existence of good. He rejects the causal theory as attributing limitations to God and concentrates on the second type of solution. He notes that it can be developed as noted above on the aesthetic model and also on a model of dynamic progress. His discussion then proceeds by distinguishing first order, second order, and third order evils and goods.[18]

First order evils are pain and suffering. Mackie notes the corresponding goods, pleasure and happiness. (There are other first order goods such as knowledge, aesthetic enjoyment and excellence, rationality, and the like, which Mackie does not mention and which he may deny to be such). Second order goods such as generosity, benevolence, pity, courage, arise in complex situations in which first order evil is said to be a necessary component. Mackie accepts that evils of the first order are logically necessary for the second order goods. In fact what is necessary is not the existence of the evil but a belief in the existence of evils of the first order kind for most of the second order goods noted here to occur. (It may well be argued that the belief can occur in the cases of some of the evils only if the reality occurs, and further, that such false belief would itself be another kind of evil which called for explanation and justification. This is not unimportant if true, for false belief in the existence of such evils is a much lesser evil than the evils themselves). Mackie notes three possible lines of reply to such a solution. Firstly he notes that it might be argued that second order goods are only derivatively good as a means to first order goods, but he chooses not to press this line of argument. I suggest that it ought to be pressed strongly as it does seem to be the case that we value benevolence, industry, determination, courage, pity, gratitude, because and in so far as they are useful, and because they involve an attitude of good will or respect for our fellow men. The latter attitude of respect and good will is possible between happy, contented, virtuous men. Thus, where not useful, we should simply prize good will and integrity and them alone of these goods. Pity is an ugly thing. Gratitude is somewhat ugly and can be positively debasing; and it is an unfortunate character-trait for a person to have to crave gratitude. However, as indicated, Mackie simply notes but does not develop this line of reply. Secondly, it follows from this solution that God cannot possess the attributes of benevolence and sympathy so often ascribed to him. God's concern is simply to promote goods of the second order rather than to minimise evils of the first order.

[18] "Evil and Omnipotence", *Mind,* LXIV, 1955, pp. 200-212.

This is not a refutation but a powerful *ad hominem* consideration. Thirdly, Mackie notes that just as there are second order goods arising from first order evils, so there are second order evils, evils such as malevolence, cruelty, callousness, cowardice, and the like. If the second order goods are of an important kind of good, (indeed the important kind it is represented as being), the second order evils must also be important. Evil of this kind exists and is stressed by theists rather more than are the first order evils. Thus the pointing to second order goods is no answer to the problem of physical evil and of evil generally, for second order evils are left unexplained. Mackie argues that if an attempt is made to explain these evils by reference to third order goods, there would then be the problem of third order evils, *ad infinitum*. This fact leads theists to explain second order evils by reference to free will, a third order good which seemingly is thought not to involve third order evils. The second order evils result from man's exercise of his free will, hence God is said not to be responsible for them. Mackie here develops a number of lines of reply. Firstly he argues that God could have made us completely virtuous and free, that second-order evils are not logically necessary accompaniments of freedom; secondly he argues that if God is all-powerful, he could have interfered with evil wills and evil choices and let alone good wills and good choices. If God could not so interfere, he would not be wholly powerful; if he could and does not he is not wholly good. Mackie also notes an equivocation in the sense of the word "freedom" as it appears in this argument.

When discussing the problem of moral evil, I shall have much to say concerning the free will issue and solution. Here I propose simply to note Mackie's claims and to indicate how N. Smart sought to answer them, leaving further discussion of this question until Section B of this Chapter. None the less it is worth noting at this point that the theist's argument totally collapses if there is no such thing as free will. It is true that without free will there can be no moral evil, but if an attempt is made to explain physical evil, pain and suffering, in terms of free will and its goods, it is essential that it be shown that men possess free will.

N. Smart sought to reply to Mackie in terms of a distinction between what he calls Cosmomorphic Universes, i.e. universes in which laws comparable with the laws of our universes prevail, and Noncosmomorphic Universes, namely those in which this is not the case.[19] *Cosmomorphic Utopia A* is explained as one in which men are wholly good, in which they are never subjected to temptation, and in which because of the nature of their likes they never engage in conflict, for instance, over women. Smart

[19] "Omnipotence, Evil and Supermen".

asks of men in such a world why they should be said to be good, arguing that the usual criteria for applying moral excellence will not apply. *Cosmomorphic Utopia B* is explained as one in which circumstances always combine to make men good. Hitler, in spite of his anti-semetic impulses would fall in love with a Jewess, who presumably would reciprocate his love, and so on. Whenever anyone was subject to temptation, he would be distracted, etc. Such a world, Smart suggests, is more like a dream than a fantasy. He suggests that implicitly an appeal is being made to the need for a law-governed universe such as ours. *Cosmomorphic Utopia C* is one in which virtue results from miraculous intervention. Smart, after noting that it is hard to make sense of this supposition, observes that:

"Either we have to count rightness and wrongness as empirical differences in order to formulate a causal law here or we must confess that no strict causal laws of human behaviour could be formulated in this cosmos. The former alternative is baffling and unacceptable, whilst the latter is incompatible with determinism." [20]

In respect of Noncosmomorphic Utopia Smart claims that we do not know what sapients in such a world would be like so we are necessarily even less clear as to what is meant by calling them good. We should have to be completely agnostic about such a world. From all this Smart concludes that moral discourse is embedded in the cosmic *status quo*. It is applied to a situation where men are beings of a certain sort such that the abstract possibility that men might have been created wholly good loses its clarity when alternative possible worlds are considered.

Here I wish to note only two objections to Smart's account. The one is that in respect of Cosmomorphic Utopia A, Smart adopts the very curious and completely untenable view of moral virtue which out-Kants Kant, that virtue involves resistance to temptation – even Kant acknowledged the possibility of a holy will! Secondly, I suggest that Smart's argument must involve the claim that this is the best of all possible worlds. The objections to such arguments have been noted in Chapter 7.

Mackie in his reply to Smart observes:

"In short, the theist can give whatever interpretation he prefers to the notion of a man's freely choosing the good, but he cannot consistently say that it is empty. The critic will then claim that with this interpretation, whatever it may be, it was logically possible for God to make men such that they would always freely choose the good." [21]

And he concludes, noting again that Smart's discussion is based on an

[20] *Op. cit., Philosophy*, 1961, p. 194.
[21] "Theism and Utopia", *Philosophy*, XXXVII, 1962, p. 155.

acceptance of the thesis that free will and determinism are compatible, in the following way:

"I conclude, then, that any theist who is prepared to give some content to the phrase 'freely choose the good' can avoid the conclusion that it was logically possible for God to have made men such that they would always freely choose the good only in one of two ways. The first way is to define freedom as mere variation ((i) above); the second is to adopt an extreme indeterminism which says that the action is not determined in any way by the agent as he is ((ii) above). For a theist who wants to solve the problem of evil by reference to free will the first way is obviously useless. Once it is dismissed, Professor Smart's case collapses; there is then no way of avoiding the Utopia Thesis if you accept the Compatibility Thesis and even the mildest form of determinism. The second way is not much better; it leads the indeterminist either to the view that agents do not act, that free actions just happen, or to the view that the action of a free agent is a very mysterious business, determination by a substance *qua* substance and not through its characteristics. Of these, the former is clearly useless for theism, so that it is only by embracing the latter that a theist can deny the Utopia Thesis.

Granting that there is this one view on which the Utopia Thesis can be denied, I would add that this does not yet solve the problem of evil. For one thing, this view is hard to reconcile with the high value which the theist must place upon freedom if he is to adopt the freewill solution. For another, as I argued in my article, the freewill solution would require also that men's wills should be so free that God *cannot* control them, and this cannot be true of a God whose power is limited only by logical necessity." [22]

In reply to Mackie's mode of meeting the theist's arguments, I argued that it conceded too much to the theist, that it implicitly allowed that the problem of physical evil may be reduced to that of moral evil. Instead of, or supplementary to Mackie's reply which involves allowing the problem of pain and suffering to be translated into the single problem concerning moral evil, I wish to insist that they are separate problems and argue: (a) The aesthetic argument fails to indicate *how much* evil, pain, and suffering is necessary for and justified by the goods to which it leads, i.e. it fails to face up to Problem 2 as noted in Chapter 1. This is the point Wisdom is concerned to stress in his discussion.[23] Wisdom suggests that in view of the vast amount of pain and suffering that occurs, it is probable that there is an excess of evil. A supporting argument therefore needs to be offered

[22] *Ibid.,* pp. 157-8.
[23] "God and Evil", *Mind*, XLIV, 1935.

by the theist to show that the amount of evil which occurs is necessary for the goods which occur. No such supplementary argument is offered. (b) It is argued that evil contributes to good, but it may equally be argued that good contributes to the occurrence of evil. Theists often claim that this is so in contexts other than that of discussion of the problem of evil. Hick, in the latter context, notes the amount of evil which prevails in affluent societies in the form of suicides and the like. This means that if this sort of argument is accepted we ought to consider it dangerous both to eliminate evil and to promote good. Greater evil may come from both kinds of endeavour. This is not a serious moral standpoint to adopt. (c) The argument is completely irrelevant to many instances of pain and suffering for a vast amount of suffering passes unnoticed. Much animal pain, and much suffering in children, is of this kind. Such pain and suffering occurs – we know in general although not in detail that it occurs – yet much of such pain and suffering can have no uplifting effects in the sufferers, they being animals and young children. And, being unobserved, it can have no beneficial effects for other people in the world. This is really an elaboration of Wisdom's point that there is more pain than is necessary for the goods produced. Further to the point, much pain produces moral evils such as a sense of defeat, self-pity, selfishness, cringing, cowardice, terror. Such pain as has no second-order effects, or second-order effects such as the latter, is not justified by reference to higher goods. No doubt the theist here as elsewhere would suggest that one cannot assess individual pains and sufferings, that one has to take the package deal of all pain and suffering together with all the higher goods and evils, since pains and suffering are results of laws of nature. This still leaves unsettled where the balance lies, with evil or with good, and throws the burden of the theist's defence on the law-governed universe argument discussed under (v) above. (d) The moral judgment involved is an abominable one. As I have argued elsewhere:

"The theist's argument is seen to imply that war plus courage plus the many other moral virtues war brings into play are better than peace and its virtues; that famine and its moral virtues are better than plenty; that disease and its moral virtues are better than health." [24]

This kind of moral judgment is utterly indefensible and no sane, humane, moral agent could possibly act on the basis of it. Yet it is this very value judgment that underlies this solution.

(e) Niven and Joyce in the passages quoted above argue that pain is justified as a goad to action. This is a false generalization. Much suffering frustrates and wrecks the person as a person, destroying him completely

[24] "God and Evil", *Philosophical Quarterly,* 10, 1960, p. 108.

as a person. Secondly, many engage in their work from love of what they are doing. It is surprising to find a Jesuit suggesting the contrary. Weariness, fatigue, and the like, get in the way of the dedicated philosopher, scientist, welfare worker. Further, this argument implies that God has made us with an inbuilt laziness mechanism. This is to ascribe to God an evil of another kind, and thereby makes the problem of evil more acute. (f) The objection that the negative virtues are not of the value that this solution suggests them to be has already been noted. In practice we never hesitate to eliminite pain and suffering at the expense of lessening opportunities for pity, benevolence, and the like, and this because these virtues are largely utilitarian virtues. Some Christians actually acted in a way consistent with their value judgments and resisted the use of anaesthetics, painless childbirth, and the like, and some current Christian opposition to voluntary euthanasia has a suggestion of the same value judgment, even though it is true that a view about the taking of human life is also involved here. (g) I have argued that the highest moral excellence is to be found not in these utilitarian virtues but in a positive attitude towards one's fellow men and the world. The good man, the morally admirable man, is he who loves what is good, knowing that it is good, and preferring it because it is good. He does not need to be subject to temptation, nor torn by suffering, nor by the spectacle of another's suffering, to be morally admirable. Fortitude in his own sufferings and sympathetic kindness in others' may reveal to us his goodness, but the good man's goodness is not necessarily increased by such things.

How do these comments stand in respect of Plantinga's demand that the critic of theism must show that it is logically impossible that evil be justified? Obviously they do not measure up to Plantinga's demands. They relate to the amount of evil, and not merely to the existence of any evil; and they make reference to moral principles which are not analytic but synthetic *a priori*. The objections are none the worse for that. On the other hand, the narrowness of Plantinga's approach to the problem of evil emerges from the relevance of the solutions and replies thereto.[25]

(viii) Immortality as providing an opportunity for correcting injustices which occur in this world

Campbell, and others including Kant, have sought to explain and justify unavoidable, undeserved suffering in this world in terms of compensating joy in a future immortal existence. This at best would be an account rele-

[25] *Op. cit.*, chapters 5 and 6.

vant to human beings. It is usually not seen to be relevant to animal suffering, for few theists wish to argue for an immortal existence for animals. The cases of so-called, unavoidable, undeserved suffering which Campbell's account is intended to justify are those concerning the sufferings of young children, innocent victims of natural calamities and of diseases, and the like. Even as an account directed at this limited group of cases of undeserved suffering, it is unsatisfactory. In the human situation we do not judge compensatory goods as being such as to justify the evils concerned. Rather, we regard them as mitigating the evils. We arrange for the maimed pedestrian to be compensated for his injury; but this we deem but a second best. It would be better if he had not been injured. The compensation is all we can do to mitigate the evil. Similarly, it would be ridiculous for a person to beat up another person and then to seek to justify his behaviour by providing compensatory joy. To this it will be replied that this is not a relevant case, for it is *unavoidable* evil which is being justified by being compensated for. This is true, but the latter example brings out how the compensating of the victim is a lesser good and one which leaves much evil unjustified.

(ix) Faith as providing, not a solution, but a ground for believing that there is a solution

It is often argued as by A. Lecerf in *An Introduction to Reformed Dogmatics* that it is presumptuous and arrogant for us to try to judge God on the basis of our limited human reason.[26] How, it is asked, can beings with such limited powers as men be sufficiently confident of their reasonings to claim that God is either imperfect or does not exist. There is some basis for this charge. We humans do make mistakes, and it is not unreasonable for it to be suggested that we should rely on our reasonings only when nothing better is available. This fact is recognized in the sphere of perception and in other areas and in respect of other matters. Thus, if one's efforts in map reading suggest that you are at Gundagai, and the signs indicate that you are in Wagga Wagga, you rely on the observed facts and not on your reasonings. We also acknowledge this fact where personal relationships are involved. It is not irrational to have faith in a friend and hence to believe him to be innocent, even when massive circumstantial evidence points to his guilt. This is because knowledge of character which comes from a long and intimate friendship is thought to be reliable knowledge based on inference from specific facts.

Some theists have suggested that the situation in respect of suffering

[26] London, Lutterworth Press, 1949, Appendix XI.

and faith in God is rather like that with a friend of high moral virtue who appears to be acting badly. While inference from the facts in the world does suggest that God is guilty of evil on a vast and shocking scale, the believer is nevertheless confident that God is really good. He has a superior knowledge of God. He has faith, trust, and confidence in God, based on his experience of knowing God. Faith is explained as reliance upon God, a counting on him which comes from personal knowledge. It is here suggested that there not only can be but is, in the faith relationship, a personal relationship akin to that of friendship. If knowledge of the kind that comes from long, deep, intimate friendships were possible in respect of God, such knowledge would indeed provide a basis for ceasing to regard evil as a problem. However, although Christians often speak of God as personal, and of the relationship between God and man as a personal one, such talk must for the reasons indicated earlier be metaphorical. Among the reasons for this are the facts that prayer and communion with God are not literal conversations, and that believers cannot attain insight into God's motives, intentions, and purposes in the way one friend does of the other. It is only this latter knowledge that provides reasonable grounds for faith and trust in a friend. To attain comparable knowledge of God we should first need to understand his purpose in permitting evil, for without such knowledge we should have no grounds for trusting him.

That the description of faith as personal knowledge of God is metaphorical is apparent too when we consider how certain notable theologians have interpreted faith. Calvin defined faith as "a steady and certain knowledge of the Divine benevolence towards us, which, being founded on the truth of gratuitous promise in Christ, is both revealed to our minds and confirmed to our hearts by the Holy Spirit." [27] Paul Tillich spoke of faith as the state of being ultimately concerned, as claiming truth for its concern, and as involving commitment, courage, and the taking of a risk.[28] Much the same view is expressed by Richard Niebuhr thus:

"What I have in mind is the attitude and action of confidence in, and fidelty to, certain realities as the sources of value and the objects of loyalty. This personal attitude or action is ambivalent: it involves reference to the value that attaches to the self and to the value toward which the self is directed. On the one hand, it is trust in that which gives value to the self: on the other hand, it is loyalty to what the self values." [29]

[27] *Institutes of the Christian Religion,* Philadelphia, Presbyterian Board of Religious Education, 1936, trans. J. Allen, III, 2, 7, p. 604.

[28] *The Dynamics of Faith,* London, Allen & Unwin, 1957.

[29] *Radical Monotheism and Western Culture,* Lincoln, University of Nebraska, 1960, p. 8.

Faith, so understood, is very different from knowledge. The issue here is whether faith can provide a way out of the problem of evil. It is relevant that many who, at one stage of their lives believe that they have this faith relationship with God, finally come to see that they really have been experiencing something quite different. It is also significant that the claims made among those who believe themselves to be experiencing genuine faith actually conflict with one another. The facts that faith contains no marks of its own validity, that it is so often obviously illusory, and that it admits of no testing, mean that it is irrational to rely on it against the conclusions arrived at by rational inference. It is not to be dogmatic to insist that it is more rational to rely on the less fallible and more reliable knowledge that rational inference provides than on the sort of faith that is much confused with and apparently indistinguishable from illusory faith. Niebuhr writes of people having faith in democracy, and presumably also in their democratic leaders. Such faith may be reasonable but it is so only as long as inference from the facts does not suggest that it is misdirected. The same holds in respect of faith in God.

While most claims about faith made by the faithful do not admit of outside confirmation, there is one claim made by most theologians which does admit of checking, and which, when checked, tells against faith. I refer to the claim that faith brings with it better works. A man possessed of faith in God is said to be aided in his moral life and to be morally a better person, not necessarily morally better than an unbeliever, but better than he was or would be if he himself were an unbeliever. Since many believers are converts, this claim admits of some testing. When tested it seems not to be confirmed. Sometimes no doubt the person involved does change, but his total moral stature seems no better. Of course the rejoinder might be made that these are not cases of genuine faith. Yet if the possessor can be so deceived by illusory faith as this suggestion would imply, the initial objection above gains force.

There is further ground for doubting the validity of the claim made for faith. If faith is really a matter of trusting in and knowing God, one would reasonably expect that it would not merely make its possessors better than they were, but better than other men. Such commitment, trust, and knowledge, if they are as they are represented as being, ought to provide a great incentive and boost to their moral endeavours. That this is not obviously the case only confirms the suspicion that all faith may be illusory and misdirected.

If faith is understood as something that improves our moral life, it simply makes the problem of moral evil more acute. We cannot, by an act of free will, acquire faith and grace. Many persons seem never to be offered them by God. Yet, by granting faith in those who wish to know and rely on the truth, God could increase the amount of moral virtue and reduce the amount of moral evil. In fact, if he exists, he appears to allow avoidable moral evil to occur. The objections noted above suggest that faith can no more be used to explain or justify this moral evil than it can be used as a basis for overcoming the problem of suffering.

I therefore contend that faith is not an aid to the theist in his attempt to solve the problem of evil. It would offer a way out only if it were a superior way of knowing, a way of knowing of the kind which may come with a deep, long-standing personal friendship, and hence, something confirmed by experience and knowledge of a person's actions, motives, and intentions. Faith in that sense rarely is claimed to occur. In the presence of the fact of evil, it cannot occur, for it demands a previous understanding of God's purposes in permitting evil, an understanding that by the very nature of the case is not available. In fact the problem of evil is aggravated by the claim that faith improves moral performance or at least is claimed to do so.

(x) The agnostic position, that we cannot know that there is not a solution, and that it cannot be shown that a solution is logically impossible

These contentions have already been touched on in Chapter 1 and discussed more fully in Chapter 6. Here it will be sufficient to set out how our contentions and conclusions relate to these claims. Concerning M. B. Ahern's claim that evil may be a logically necessary condition for goods, and that the goods may provide a justification for permitting the evils to occur, it was agreed that this is *in principle* true. However, it was denied that this holds of God, and this for two reasons. The one relates to the nature of the goods pointed to by Ahern. The goods must be such as to be logically and not simply causally dependent on evils. The goods which are such and which are cited as such seem not to be intrinsic goods, whereas the more obvious intrinsic goods, the goods rightly most highly prized, are not logically dependent on the existence of evils. Compare here goods such as compassion, sympathy, fortitude, gratitude, endurance, and industry, on the one hand, and pleasure, happiness, beauty, knowledge, rationality, self-perfection and friendship and love, on the other. God, being omnipotent, can bring about greater good in the form of the latter goods without in any way resorting to causing or permitting evil of any kind to exist. In respect of the problem concerning actual evil, it is possible to set out the ethical connecting link in some such form as 'An all-perfect being would not permit avoidable, unjustified evil'. The issue then becomes that discussed for the greater part of Section A concerning the plausibility of attempts to show that actual evil is either not avoidable or not unjustified. No deductive argument to show that a solution is impossible can successfully be attempted. Rather we have to be guided as to whether the weight of evidence suggests that the apparent contradiction is more, or less, probably a real contradiction. Another point concerning actual evil is relevant here. If the actual evil found in the world includes cruel and barbarous attempts to exterminate a racial group, or if it involves the slow, lingering deaths of many from malnutrition and starvation, to suggest that because evils can be justified by reference to goods for which they are logically necessary conditions, and to wonder what kinds and how much such goods would be necessary to justify these evils, is to misunderstand the nature of the argument. The critic of theism may wish to suggest that the probability of such evils really being justified is so slight that a contradiction is almost certainly involved in the joint assertion 'An all-perfect being exists' and 'These kinds of evils exist,' or he may be appealing to a synthetic *a priori* moral principle and saying that it is the nature of the case that goods cannot justify such evils. To reply, as does Plantinga, that a solution is logically possible, to reproach the critics of theism as he does Mackie and myself, because we do not explore every logically conceivable solution, including that to the effect that the evils may be due to evil spirits, is to miss the point of the argument here.[30] It is not necessary for the critic to explore whether evil spirits, mischievous fairies, clumsy Homeric gods, or the like, can be shown possibly to be the cause of certain kinds of evils. This is to rest the theist's case on a purely skeptical, unreal doubt. Indeed, Plantinga's wholly negative approach along the lines that the atheologian has failed to show that a solution is logically impossible

---

[30] *Op. cit.*, chapters 5 and 6. An even more ingenious apologist than Plantinga might seek to keep open the possibility of a solution by means of the legitimate although desperate move that the moral judgments upon which the problems rest, namely that pain and suffering are evils, that the deliberate and unnecessary infliction of suffering and the like on innocent persons is evil, are not analytic but synthetic judgments and hence that the problem cannot logically be shown not to admit of a solution. I should wish to argue that the value judgments upon which the problem of evil rests, particularly Problem 2 which is that which arouses most concern, are synthetic necessary moral judgments – that pain and suffering are evils seem very evidently not to be analytic judgments. Yet if this is so, it follows that the atheologian cannot ever show that a solution to Problem 2 is impossible, logically impossible. It is true that Problem 1 can be stated without any content being given to evil, its nature, but this rarely occurs.

suggests the same insensivity as to the reality of the issues and problems involved as does Leibniz's discussion, and is in marked contrast with the deeply concerned approaches of philosophers such as Joyce, Journet, and Campbell. A test of the earnestness of one who adopts Plantinga's mode or argument consists in seeing whether he is prepared to allow preventable evil to continue because if he does not intervene say to save a child from being burnt alive, the evil he does not prevent may be justified since the atheologian cannot show that a justification of it is logically impossible.

SECTION B – MORAL EVIL

Stating the Problem

As I argued in "God and Evil," the theist must interpret moral evil not simply as moral fault but as being or involving a breach of God's law, and a rejection of God himself. Thus in creating beings capable of moral evil, and in creating them with the foreknowledge that they would engage in moral evil, God created beings whom he knew would infringe his law, reject him by engaging in such evil actions as lying, cheating, being unkind to others, being callous, cruel, injuring their fellow men and killing and torturing them, showing spite, exhibiting jealousy, feeling envy, and manifesting all the unpleasant traits we know that we ourselves and our fellow men can manifest in the daily course of everyday life, and doing so, often. Many Christians recite in their prayers, the words "Forgive us our trespasses" daily. They also pray "Almighty and most merciful Father, we have erred and strayed from thy ways like lost sheep. We have followed too much the devices and desires of our own hearts. We have offended against thy holy laws." This prayer too is commonly recited daily. Sin, moral evil, is not thought to be something rare and unusual. It is thought to be a commonplace and most theists think that all men, or all with rare exceptions, are sinners who sin often. Such is the case with the ordinary person. As we well know, there are extraordinarily evil men, the Hitlers, the Stalins, the Eichmanns, the professional murderers, and the like. Hence it is that when considering moral evil, we find that the amount of moral evil which has to be explained and justified is immense. This had led some philosophers to overlook that among the problems raised by the fact of moral evil, there are two problems, and not simply the one, concerning the compatibility of moral evil and God's perfection. There is the traditional, almost purely academic problem concerning the reconciliation of the occurrence of *any* moral evil with God's claim to perfection, and that concerned with the *actual* moral evil which occurs, the kinds and amounts of moral evil. It is because of the reality and immensity of the evil which poses the latter problem that the former problem tends to be ignored or dismissed as unimportant. It is important to the extent that if any, some, one instance of moral evil were to be shown to be incompatible with the divine perfection, it would thereby have been shown that the actual moral evil which occurs is incompatible with it. Our main concern however will be with proposed solutions which relate to the actual moral evil that occurs.

Relevant to the problem posed by actual moral evil is the fact that besides being an evil in itself, the evil of the rejection of God himself according to the theist, moral evil usually increases the amount of physical evil in the world. Some theists seem to wish to argue that the greater amount of physical evil is caused by man himself. This however is not true, although it is true that a vast amount of pain and suffering is caused by human beings who engage in morally evil actions. A vast amount is also caused by well-intentioned, misguided actions of men, men like the Inquisitors, the Puritans, and puritanical Christians and the like. Also relevant is the fact that according to many forms of theism those who engage in morally evil acts suffer punishment for them, the traditional Christian view being that many suffer eternal punishment in the form of torment for their morally evil acts. Thus God, in knowingly creating beings who would engage in morally evil acts, consented to moral evil, the physical evils which these moral evils caused, and, if the part of Christian orthodoxy relating to Hell be accepted, also to the eternal damnation, i.e. suffering of the damned. Thus the problem posed by actual moral evil is no small one.

Proposed Solutions

The solutions that have been proposed have been in terms of the value of free will, the value of free will *and* the goods that freedom makes to be possible and actual, or simply in terms of the good or goods freedom makes to be actual. A range of statements of exponents of such solutions will serve to illustrate the character of the proposed solutions.

"The existence of moral evil, however, becomes explicable, when it is admitted that man's life is a probation. ... God, in other words, has created the present order such that man should have the glory of meriting his last end. We can see readily enough that in this He has conferred a great privilege upon us. To receive our final beatitude as the fruit of our labours, and as the recompense of a hard-won victory, is an incomparably higher destiny than to receive it without any effort on our part. And since God in His wisdom has seen fit to give us such a lot as this, it was inevitable that man should have the power to choose the wrong. We could not be called to merit the reward due to victory without being exposed to the possibility of defeat." [31]

"God is able not to create free beings, but if he does create them they will be able to fall away." [32]

"From the moment that created persons are naturally peccable, there will be some who will in fact sin; and even, if it is a question of human beings after original sin, all will sin to some extent or other, except in Heaven. Hence we must conclude that in fact God would not have created nature if he had not ordained it to grace and to that charity by which man becomes, under grace, freely the friend of God, and that sin is the ransom of glory." [33]

"Without fallible freedom there can be no created freedom; without created freedom there can be no love in mutual friendship between God and Creature; without love in mutual friendship between God and creature, there can be no supernatural transformation of the creature into God. Sin – evil, – is the price of glory." [34]

Writing of the traditional free will defence of moral evil, J. Hick writes:

"To this question the Christian answer, both in the Augustinian and in the Irenaean types of theodicy, has always centred upon man's freedom and responsibility as a finite personal being." [35]

Free Will Alone as a Complete Solution

The argument here is along the lines that men have free wills, that moral evil is a consequence of the exercise of free will, that a universe in which there are beings who possess free will, even though it be with lapses into moral evil, is better than one in which men are automata, doing good always because predetermined to do so. Thus the argument would be that it is the value of free will alone which justifies God's allowing moral evil and all the physical evils that moral evil and the punishments for moral evil may involve.

In reply to such an argument it might first be asked why, if freedom is such a good, it is not more generously distributed. Animals are thought

[31] Joyce, *Op. cit.*, pp. 600-1.
[32] Journet, *Op. cit.*, p. 149.
[33] J. Maritain, *God and the Permission of Evil*, p. 37.
[34] J. Maritain, *St. Thomas and the Problem of Evil*, p. 19. See p. 99 above.
[35] *Op cit.*, p. 301.

not to possess it, and many human beings are acknowledged not to possess it. Infants who are born to suffer and to die in childhood never enjoy it. We lose it in extreme old age with senility, and many such as the insane have never possessed it or have permanently lost it. Such a great boon as free will is represented as being is much less widely enjoyed than one would expect on the hypothesis of there being an all-powerful, omniscient, benevolent creator. My belief is that the appeal to free will makes the existence of animals with all the suffering they endure, and endure simply because they lack free will, an immensely greater problem than it otherwise would be. Why then, it must be asked, has the boon of free will been restricted to human beings, and even then, to simply the majority of them? (This is to accept uncritically for the moment that human beings possess free will. This is presupposed in accepting the problem of moral evil as a real problem.) There is a suggestion of arbitrariness in the claim that free will is such a great good (and that the goods to which it gives rise are so valuable), that God confined the possession of it to so few of his creations. Why should not dogs, cats, horses, and apes, as well as a multitude of other animals enjoy free will? Obviously they would avoid many avoidable evils, were they to possess free will.

Theists who appeal to the free will solutions to the problem of moral evil not uncommonly do not bother to attempt to show that human beings in fact possess free will. They seem simply to assume this. Of course, they are justified in this to the extent that the problem of moral evil arises as a problem only on the hypothesis that there are free agents who sin, who morally err. If the "immoral act" were not a free act it would not be truly immoral. Were we not free there would be no problem of moral evil, as moral evil is properly understood. Instead, there would be the distinct problem for the theist concerning why God created beings preordained to engage in all the vile "acts" in which men, so-called free agents, engage. It would be the problem of explaining evils comparable with that of the lion which tears the giraffe to pieces as it slowly dies in agony; it would be the problem of explaining why God created beings as subtle and clever as man, with a consciousness of what they are doing, and who commonly suffer feelings of guilt, horror, and remorse, when in fact if they lack free will they have been preordained to do what they do. Unless it can be shown that men truly have free will, the problem of physical evil is vastly worsened, and many proposed solutions of the latter problem fall apart. If man lacks free will, there can be no moral evil in the understood sense. Equally there can be no moral good. Heroism, courage, benevolence, integrity, and the like, become things without moral character or excellence; men will be simply automata, imperfect automata, who believe that they have free will and suffer feelings of weakness, guilt, remorse, distress, anguish, as well as pride, joy, a sense of achievement, that they ought not and do not deserve to feel. Thus if we are not free agents, and yet have been created so as to believe that we are free and so as to experience the suffering that this belief brings in its wake, the problem of suffering becomes more acute.

It is not possible here to enter into a discussion as to whether we do or do not possess free will. Instead I simply note what follows if we lack freedom, namely that there would be no problem of moral evil but a more perplexing problem of physical evil. I shall assume that free will is incompatible with complete determinism, but in various contexts will briefly consider what would follow if it could be shown that free will and determinism are compatible.

If we are free, our freedom is far from complete freedom. At best it is a limited, restricted, imperfect freedom. Clearly, even if it could successfully be established that we are free agents, there would remain the very considerable problem that if freedom is the great good that theists represent it as being, we possess it very imperfectly, and many possess it not at all – consider here the insane, the mental defectives, the compulsives, and the like. Stupidity, indeed any imperfection of reason which makes us lack complete, perfect rationality is a limitation on freedom. If we make mistakes and do not achieve what we seek to achieve we are not fully free. So too, ignorance is a limitation on freedom. To choose course A which leads to what we do not want, rather than course B, because we do not know and cannot possibly come to know that it leads to what we do not want, and when course B does achieve what we desire, is to be in a state of unfreedom. A person or being is not fully free unless fully rational, omniscient – factually and morally – and unless able to achieve what he chooses to achieve. Human beings, by virtue of their limitations, their finitude, and even more by virtue of the special imperfections and defects as individual persons, lack full freedom. What we possess is a very imperfect, defective substitute. This means that much so-called moral evil is not really morally evil conduct. It also means that no human being can make a fully free, human response of the kind theists commonly claim can and does occur in respect of God's love. Unavoidable foolishness, ignorance, moral error, the limitations placed on individuals by their environment, nature, heredity, and the like, are real limitations on freedom. Only an omniscient, fully rational, omnipotent being would/can be completely free, for freedom in the morally relevant sense consists in being fully responsible for one's choices and actions, in one's actions being fully one's own. In brief, it is arguable whether human persons possess free will, but if they do, they possess it in a very limited, restricted way. And not all possess even this limited degree of freedom.

The next issue which arises here is whether the freedom that persons are reasonably claimed to possess is or is not compatible with their being biassed to good. Here three distinct considerations may be noted. Firstly, when acknowledging that greater, more perfect freedom than man enjoys is possible, Aquinas, in noting that angels possess greater or more perfect freedom so explains this freedom in terms of its more readily leading to good. He wrote:

"Free will in its choice of means to an end is disposed just as the intellect is to its conclusions. Now it is evident that it belongs to the power of the intellect to be able to proceed to different conclusions, according to given principles; but for it to proceed to some conclusion by passing out of order of the principles, comes of its own defect. Hence it belongs to the perfection of its liberty for free-will to be able to choose between opposite things, keeping the order of the end in view; but it comes of the defect of liberty for it to choose anything by turning away from the order of the end; and this is to sin. Hence there is greater liberty of will in the angels, who cannot sin, than there is in ourselves, who can sin." [36]

Further, original sin is claimed to have corrupted man so that he will sin; and the Thomistic formula, that among peccable beings some must fail, suggests that there can be freedom and yet bias, inevitable bias, towards sin. Again, man is made with various desires, for food, drink, sexual satisfaction, desire to reproduce, for companionship, to preserve his life, and the like. When hungry, we incline to eat; when thirsty to drink; when our lives are threatened we seek to protect ourselves; and so on. Our desires, unless they reach a pitch at which they become uncontrollable, do not deprive us of our freedom even though they constantly influence our conduct. This being so, the question arises whether God could not have made man with an inbuilt desire to be good, benevolent, to love his fellow man. If such desires were like our present desires, they would not deprive us of our freedom; they would simply bias us to the good whilst leaving the free choice as to what we shall do, to us. Here the argument may be put in the form of a dilemma: 'Either the present desires deprive us of freedom or they do not. If they do, we are not now fully free, and the theist's problem is one distinct from or additional to that of moral evil. If the present desires do not deprive us of freedom, and yet influence or

[36] *Summa Theologiae*, 1, 62, 8, ad. 3.

bias us towards certain modes of conduct, other good-causing desires are possible. In this event, less moral evil would have been compatible with free will or with the limited free will which we are claimed now to possess.' Here it is probable that the argument from the world being a law-governed one, and one which is better than other possible, law-governed and non-law-governed universes, in which man evolved as he is, will again be invoked to suggest that such changes in human nature as have been indicated here, are not real options open to God. The same reply is available as that indicated in our discussion of the laws of nature argument in Section A, (v).

It has been argued that not simply less evil but that a complete absence of evil (as opposed to complete virtue) is compatible with the possession of freedom of the will, that God could have created men possessing free will and who never sinned. Relevant here are saints, angels and God himself, and, on the human plain, those who truly love, love in a completely disinterested way, another person. To consider the latter case first. It has rightly been noted by many that in a happy marriage each partner may be completely free to commit adultery, yet neither could possibly do so. Yet they act freely in abstaining from adultery. Why then, given the love a man may have for God and for his fellow men, could not men be so made as never to incline to evil but to incline instead to a love of acts which are good? That there is no obstacle in terms of possession of freedom is suggested by Aquinas in the above quotation, and again by G. H. Joyce who noted:

"And all who accept the Christian revelation admit that those who have attained their final beatitude exercise freedom of the will and yet cannot choose aught but what is truly good. They possess the knowledge of Essential Goodness: and to it, not simply to the good in general, they refer every choice. Moreover, even in our present condition, it is open to omnipotence so to order our circumstances, and to confer on the will such instinctive impulses, that we should in every election adopt the right course and not the wrong course." [37]

The world, and life in this world, are of finite duration. Heaven is for eternity. Sin is alleged not to be possible in heaven yet it is believed that it will be peopled by finite, free agents.

A further *ad hominem* argument, and one with important implications, is that from God's freedom and perfection. God not only does not sin; he cannot sin. Why then cannot this hold also of man? If free will in God is compatible with necessitation to virtue, then free will anywhere, wherever

[37] *Op. cit.*, p. 600.

it occurs, ought to be compatible with absolute virtue. This is urged here as an *ad hominem* argument and not as one which is necessarily objectively valid. This is because of the difficulties in the way of reconciling God's necessitation to virtue with his freedom and omnipotence. Presumably, God is incapable of evil because he is by nature wholly good. In other words, his nature is completely biassed to good because Being is good and he is being. Given his nature he cannot do evil. In a sense, to be a worshipful being, to be a being whom we must unconditionally obey, and one to whom we rightly yield our wills in unconditional obedience, he must be one on whom we can count absolutely not to will what is evil. We can so count on him only if he is necessarily and not simply contingently good. Thus God as God must be necessitated to virtue, yet to be perfect, he must be a free agent. If the problem of reconciling these two things, necessitation to virtue and freedom can be overcome in the case of God, they ought to admit of being overcome with lesser beings too. As an *ad hominem* argument, this argument has value. As an objective, unconditional argument, its claims are less clearly unqualified. It may simply show that the notion of an all-perfect being is an incoherent one.

Plantinga in his discussion in *God and Other Minds* rejects the contention that God could have made wholly virtuous, free persons.[38] A careful examination of his discussion reveals that it rests on a number of serious confusions. Plantinga seems to confuse predictability and unfreedom, randomness and freedom. More importantly, he also confuses the notion of "bringing about" with that of "causing". Clearly, to be unfree is distinct from being predictable. The arguments here are too well known to require repeating. So too, as Campbell and other libertarians have brought out, to be free is for the action to be solely caused by oneself, where there are genuine alternative actions possible. This is very different from randomness. Similarly, to cause someone to act in a certain way, where the causality is incompatible with free choice, is very different from *bringing it about* that an individual acts in a certain way. An able preacher can bring it about that some of his flock testify to Christ. An able teacher will bring it about that his students become interested in the subject on which he is lecturing and even that some accept his conclusions. A host may bring it about that his guest drinks a cold glass of beer by placing one beside him on a hot day. And a girl may bring it about that a boy loses attention in a lecture by flirtatiously eyeing him. In none of these cases is the person affected *caused* to act as he does. One further illustration is sufficient here. Compare the example of drinking of the beer, with the different example

[38] Chapter 6.

of the beer being put before an alcoholic who has been starved of alcohol. In the latter case I should be prepared to say that the host caused the man to drink the beer. Causing and bringing it about are different notions. We can bring about something by causing it to occur; but we can do so too without causing it. If pursued further, this issue would involve us in the question of whether reasons are causes. We need not proceed that far. The theists' notion of free will rests on a distinction between reasons and acting on reasons, and causes and acting as a result of causes.

The attempt to justify the existence of moral evil in terms of freedom ultimately rests on a value judgment concerning freedom, that the existence of free beings is of such a value as to outweigh the evils of moral evil and the physical evils to which moral evils give rise. It is here that this mode of justifying moral evil is most vulnerable. The valuation given to free will is one which does not stand up to close examination.

Before we can consider the question of the value of freedom, it is important that the sense of freedom that is relevant here be made clear. A lot of confusion in theistic writings, as is evident from the above comments concerning Plantinga and from Mackie's comments concerning Smart's discussion, is due to a failure to attend to this aspect of the problem. The sense of freedom which is relevant is that according to which we speak of free beings as beings who are self-determining. This statement is less clear than it might at first sight seem to be. In a weak sense of self-determination, the young child as much as the mature adult is self-determining or can be self-determining. He can make his own choices, make or ruin his life on the basis of them. We do not allow the child to do so because we believe that in another more significant sense of self-determination, he is incapable of determining his life because he lacks the rational ability, the control over his desires, the knowledge and the foresight, necessary for a person to know what he is doing. Self-determination involves our controlling and determining our destinies. The child, the fool, the uninformed, the weak, even when they act on the basis of their choices, are not fully self-determining because as a result of their choices, they get what they wished not to get, they fail to achieve the ends they seek to achieve, and more generally, far from being masters of their own destinies, they are playthings of outside influences. Thus it is freedom in the sense of controlling our destinies, determining the character of our lives, that is relevant here. Such freedom involves rationality, knowledge, imagination, insight. It is important to stress this distinction between the weak and the strong senses of self-determination, for freedom in the weak sense of self-determination seems to have no value in itself. It is valued for the opportunities it provides for the exercise of self-determination in the stronger sense of that expression, and for the goods that accrue from it. Thus to attribute the weaker sense of self-determination to the theist would be to weaken his case more than it ought to be weakened. The stronger sense of self-determination obviously has greater claim to be considered a good. However, the more that is read into the concept of freedom, the fewer the number of persons who can be attributed freedom. There is therefore a dilemma here. The weaker the sense of freedom attributed to persons, the more persons there will be who can be attributed freedom, but what is possessed will be of little value. On the other hand, the tighter the account given of freedom, the fewer the number of people who will possess it. Hence the problem of explaining the evil acts of the semi-free, semi-automata will be greater, but so too, greater will be the value of the freedom enjoyed by those who engage in genuinely free acts.

We may now consider the value of freedom more directly, firstly, freedom in the weak sense noted above. This is the freedom evident in the actions of children, the foolish, and the ditherers. It is exercised whenever an individual makes a choice which is not a compulsive one. Thus if a child seeks to win love and attention from his parents by playing noisily and succeeds only in irritating them, he is exercising his freedom, albeit with completely unintended results. If I decide to engage in self-medication, for example, to stop my hair thinning, and as a result render myself immediately and permanently bald, I have been self-determining. The clumsy thief who seeks easy money by robbing a rich man's house and who is caught in the act due to his carelessness is also exercising self-determination in this sense of self-determination. What then is the value of self-determination so understood? Does the fact that the decision was taken by the agent concerned add anything to the value of the situation? It would seem not. Certainly if it does, it adds something of very little value, something which lacks the supreme value that freedom must have to serve as a justification for moral evil and for all the physical evils that moral evil causes. These observations lead on to a more basic question, that concerning whether we can properly speak as do the theists of the value of freedom or of free will in the abstract. Freedom seems to be affected by the complexes into which it enters, it making some actions worse than they would be if they were not free actions. Other actions are vastly better for being free acts; and others again seem neither better nor worse for being free acts. This consideration holds in a more obvious way in respect of the stronger sense of self-determination. It none the less holds and can easily be shown to hold in respect of the weak sense of self-determination, by considering the various examples noted above. With the thief, it is clear that the action of stealing is worse for its being a free rather than a compulsive one. In the example relating to self-medication, the act again is worse for being one of avoidable stupidity. In the example of the child, it makes little difference whether the act is free or not. All cases of freedom which make the action better for being free seem to be those of freedom which involve rational judgment, foresight, intelligence, and the like, that is, actions which involve freedom in the stronger sense. Yet freedom in this sense can make evil actions vastly more evil for being freely and rationally chosen. Consider the morally virtuous action of one who risks his life to save his friends, knowing full well what he is doing. His action is all the better for being thoughtfully and reasonably chosen. So too, the cold, calculated murderer is much more evil than is the man who kills in a passion. Compare here the clever, cold-blooded murderer who slowly poisons his victim, with the man who kills his wife's lover when in a jealous rage.

I suggest therefore that freedom cannot properly be assessed in the abstract although it is true that well-exercised freedom in the strong sense of self-determination may enrich a person's life. To this it will no doubt be replied that it is not freedom that is being alluded to in this kind of solution but existence as a free agent and that life as a free, self-determining agent is of immensely and immeasurably greater value than life as an automaton. Clearly this is the claim that underlies this solution, but it is one which is exposed to the difficulty of assessing the value of a free agent *vis-a-vis* life as an automaton. The considerations noted above bear on this. There would appear to be no real reason to believe that freedom ought to be judged to be of such immense value that its value outweighs all the evils to which it does or may give rise.

There is a long tradition of political thought, and one which continues to prevail in the Western World today, according to which freedom is valued in the abstract, and yet its exponents are prepared to sacrifice freedom for happiness, justice and other goods. This might suggest that freedom can be and is properly valued in the abstract, and that when so valued, it is seen to be an immense good. This is not so. The fact that we deem it right to curtail freedom for the sake of other goods, and more commonly, to prevent evils such as pain and suffering, (witness the laws against cruelty to animals), suggests that the more apparent valuation of freedom is misleading, that we do in fact evaluate it in the particular context, and that when it is ill-used to promote evils, we commonly prefer to prevent the evil than to safeguard the freedom. For the purposes of the argument here it is sufficient to press the weaker claim that if freedom can be judged to have intrinsic value, its value would have to be deemed to be such as to justify all the evils to which it gives rise. Few are prepared to assent to such a judgment. This is confirmed by our readiness to curtail the area of our self-determination by law to achieve goods and to prevent the very kinds of evils to which this freedom is claimed to give rise and to justify. For example, we freely deprive ourselves of the freedom to be self-determining, to get drunk and drive when drunk, to prevent the misery of human suffering which comes from accidents due to drunken driving. Many other examples could be cited here including the many limitations on liberty accepted by Mill and other liberals for the sake of preventing evils. Alternatively, if self-determination cannot be valued in the abstract (and this is my contention) then it would have to be the goods of freedom which would provide the justification of moral evil and the evils it brings in its wake. This involves a very different mode of justifying moral evil, that in terms of the goods freedom makes to be possible.

Moral Evil as Justified by the Goods Freedom makes to be Possible

The goods pointed to here include various of the moral virtues, benevolence, courage, fortitude, sympathy, compassion, and the like, and goods such as victory after a struggle, union with God, a freely loving response to God's love.

The first point of importance here is that many exponents of this argument claim that free agents cannot be necessitated or attuned to complete virtue. This means that for them it must be a real possibility that any given free agent will perform only evil acts; and that this will hold of any group of free agents including all future free agents. Thus what has to be shown here is that sufficient goods which have freedom as their precondition do or will occur so as to justify the moral evils and their attendant physical evils. It requires to be shown that when the final reckoning at the end of the existence of free human beings is made, that the kinds and amounts of goods will outweigh, morally outweigh, the evils which result from the exercise of freedom. This is an impossible enterprise for the theist to attempt. We cannot possibly know how the present generation will act. We are even less capable of knowing how people will act in a century's time. The data available to us is too scanty to allow even the formulation of tentative hypotheses. This is partly due to the consideration noted by Kant, namely, that we can never be certain concerning our own and other people's motives; many an apparently disinterested act is really a calculated, selfish act. The difficulty is partly due to the very limited period

of time men have existed as free moral agents. We have too little knowledge to provide an adequate basis for a sound scientific prediction, the
prediction involving as it would, detailed knowledge about changes in
the world, in standards of living, the uses to which our scientific knowledge
will be put, and the like. Thus, I suggest that this mode of attempting to
solve the problem of moral evil is doomed at the outset. It proceeds on the
basis of, and consists wholly in a claim concerning values based on a fac-
tual claim which cannot possibly be substantiated.

For many theists the position is even more difficult than this. Many
believe in an after-life in which there are rewards and punishments. Such
theists are committed to reckoning up not merely the totals of moral goods
and their consequent physical goods and evils and the moral evils and their
consequent physical evils and goods in this world, but also the totality of
goods and evils in the immortal existence. These facts no doubt constitute
the reason theists such as J. Hick and others do not offer a philosophical
solution to the problem of evil. When faced with this problem they abandon their philosophical arguments and make appeals to revelation. They
seem to assume that there is a solution and often with not a little ingenuity
and on the basis of various theological doctrines, they set out what they
believe the solution to be.

Hick's treatment of the problem of evil is a good illustration of this.
Hick offers a package deal solution to the problem of evil. Animal pain
and suffering (in so far as they are acknowledged), carnivorism, and to
some extent, human pain and suffering are justified by reference to the
evolutionary process and the emergence of man as a free agent. The
burden of his account of the unjust distribution of human pain and suffering, as well as his account of moral evil, are in terms of free will and
the particular goods it makes to be possible. Such is the value Hick attributes to free will and its goods, he is prepared to argue that a random,
gravely unjust distribution of suffering is dictated by these goods. Here
he argues:

"It seems, then, that in a world that is to be the scene of compassionate
love and self-giving for others, suffering must fall upon mankind with
something of the haphazardness and iniquity that we now experience. It
must be apparently unmerited, pointless, and incapable of being morally
rationalized." [39]

What is said to justify this and all other evil is the good of man's free
and loving response to God's love. This special love relationship is claimed

[39] *Op. cit.*, p. 370.

to be such that it could not occur in any context other than that containing evil. To this point, Hick explains:

"Man's 'fallenness' is thus the price paid for his freedom as a personal being in relation to the personal Infinite. God is so overwhelmingly great that the children in His heavenly family must be prodigal children who have voluntarily come to their Father from a far country, prompted by their own need and drawn by His love." [40]

Hick's account is completed by a rejection of the orthodox Christian belief in Hell, and by an acceptance of a belief in Purgatory, a Purgatory in which all sinners finally come to this loving relationship with God. No philosophical arguments are offered in support of Hick's belief in immortality, in Heaven, and in Purgatory. These crucial elements of his solution are presented as facts not needing philosophical justification. Even so Hick would appear to be fully exposed to the criticisms levelled at Leibniz, that this solution commits him to the claim that this is the best possible world. It is also exposed to the difficulty noted in Chapter 4, concerning the sense in which God could be said to respond to man's love, with his love. More basic, the value judgment involved is an incredible one. The suggestion that an all-perfect being could achieve this love-relationship only at this cost, and that it is worth the cost, bear greater credit to Hick's zeal than to his humanity.

By contrast with the solution offered by Hick to the problem of evil, that of G. H. Joyce in *Principles of Natural Theology* is a thoughtful, sensitive, and to an extent, a tentative one. Joyce, like Hick, seeks a solution in terms of the goods that free will makes to be possible. He argues:

"God, in other words, has created the present order such that man should have the glory of meriting his last end. We can see readily enough that in this He has conferred a great privilege upon us. To receive our final beatitude as the fruit of our labours and as the recompense of a hard-won victory, is an incomparably higher destiny than to receive it without any effort on our part. ... We could not be called to merit the reward due to victory without being exposed to the possibility of defeat." [41]

Joyce then goes on to acknowledge that not simply is there a possibility of defeat but that often there is actual defeat. This means that for Joyce there is purposeless moral evil which results in the physical evil of Hell. This leads Joyce to consider whether it might not have been better if there had simply been the struggle and no defeats, he acknowledging that God as an omnipotent being could have arranged this. Joyce's reply is that a

[40] *Ibid.*, p. 359.
[41] *Op. cit.*, p. 603.

struggle without the real possibility of defeat, that is, a struggle where it is antecedently certain that however a man may bear himself, God would bring it about that he should be saved from ultimate disaster, would be a mock struggle. However, he is not happy with this as a proposed solution, since, for the theist who believes in God's omnipotence, the defeats and the victories are antecedently certain for God, and hence the battles, mock battles. Joyce does not indicate this, but rather argues that for God to abstain from creating those who will be defeated or to remove the possibility of defeat would be for him to allow his design to be limited by human weakness. God must base his design on perfect wisdom and perfect goodness. Thus Joyce writes:

"None can reasonably dispute that an order of things in which beatitude is conferred on man as the reward of personal effort is not merely compatible with the Divine goodness, but exhibits that attribute in an altogether singular degree. And it would appear that the permission of moral evil, and even of final loss, is an inevitable condition of such a system." [42]

Joyce then draws an analogy between moral development which comes against the background of opposition of moral evil and the lion drawing its life from that of its victim. The moral evil is represented as being equally essential for the development towards moral perfection and towards the good of those who are faithful to the moral law. Thus, in brief, Joyce's solution involves the claim that the evils of moral evil, the physical evil consequent upon moral evil, Hell, are all justified by the attaining of beatitude by some, by merit after a struggle, and that God could not have attained this final end by means which involved less evil.

In reply it may be asked how the final outcome can be known with such confidence, how it can be assumed that the balance of goods over evils will be sufficiently great as to justify the evils. Joyce seems simply to assume that there will be sufficient persons to come to enjoy beatitude to justify all the evils that will occur. Further, given God's foreknowledge of successes and failures, there is the problem of the justification of the moral judgment which allows such a world to come into being, and this even if a majority were foreseen to triumph. When one looks at how the struggle is weighted against so many, for example, those from criminal homes, those living in abject poverty, those reared without love and care, Joyce's claim that those who err forgo the right to be treated as ends, is seen to be harsh, and one which clashes with much Christian thought and teaching. When one considers the untold misery caused to innocent beings in this life by the morally evil acts of others, and the abominable character

[42] *Ibid.*, p. 603.

of moral evil itself, the suffering involved in the punishment of the sinner, and presumably in his loved ones, Joyce's talk about triumphs after struggles has a touch of unreality about it. This whole morality of struggles is, I suggest, an ugly, unreal one, and one upon which we ought not to act in respect of our friends and children. It is even less morally defensible on the divine level. Consider here Joyce's claim:

"If a soul has finally chosen the road of rebellion against God, then no possibility remains that its good should be an object of Divine solicitude. From that moment it can only serve the good of others. Its fate serves as a warning to those whose probation is not yet over. And the stern sanctions of the Divine laws to which it is subject reveal to the just certain attributes of God – the rigour of His justice, and His indignation against wrong – which otherwise could not have found manifestation in the created order." [43]

Joyce alludes to the limitations of human reason, but if we approach religion philosophically, we are committed to following reason, except where reason itself directs that we do not rely on it. Our problem, as was Joyce's, is whether there is a rational, philosophical solution to the problem of evil. His comment on the limitations of human reason are designed to suggest that there may none the less be one to be found. This may indeed be the case. There is no philosophical theory in respect of which a similar theory could not be claimed to be possible. Yet, we should not respect a philosopher who withheld assent say to determinism, phenomenalism, or any other philosophical theory simply because human reason is limited and hence that the alternative theory may in fact be true.

This too is the proper reply to theistic apologists who adopt a skeptical stance in respect of discussions of the problem, for instance, Plantinga. It is true that the foregoing arguments do not establish that it is logically impossible that theists will find a solution to the problem posed by moral evil. They simply show where the weight of evidence and argument now available points.

---

[43] *Ibid.*, p. 605.

BIBLIOGRAPHY

BOOKS

Ahern, M. B. *The Problem of Evil,* London, Routledge & Kegan Paul, 1971.

Aquinas, St. Thomas *Summa Theologiae (Summa Theologica,* trans. Dominican Fathers).

Aquinas, St. Thomas *Summa Contra Gentiles,* Edition published by Doubleday & Co., New York, 1955 – various translators.

Augustine, St., Bishop of Hippo *The Enchiridion: Basic Works of St. Augustine,* New York, Random House, 1948, trans. J. F. Shaw

Boethius, *De Consolatione Philosophiae.*

Calvin, J. *Institutes of Christian Religion,* Philadelphia, Presbyterian Board of Religious Education, 1936, trans. J. Allen.

Campbell, C. A. *On Selfhood and Godhood,* London, Allen & Unwin, 1957.

Copleston, F. C. *Aquinas,* Harmondsworth, Penguin, 1955.

Dostoevsky, F. *The Brothers Karamazov,* London, Heinemann, 1945, trans. C. Garnett.

Eddy, Mary Baker *Science and Health with Key to the Scriptures,* Authorized Edition.

Flew, A. *God and Philosophy,* London, Hutchinson, 1966.

Flew, A. and MacIntyre, A. *New Essays in Philosophical Theology,* London, S.C.M., 1955.

Geach, P. *God and the Soul,* London, Routledge & Kegan Paul, 1969.

Gilson, E. *The Christian Philosophy of St. Thomas Aquinas,* London, Gollancz, 1957.

Hick, J. *Evil and the God of Love,* London, Macmillan, 1966.

Hume, D. *Dialogues Concerning Natural Religion.*

Journet, C. *The Meaning of Evil,* London, Geoffrey Chapman, 1963, trans. M. Barry.

Joyce, G. H. *Principles of Natural Theology,* London, Longmans, Green & Co., 3rd. edition 1923, new impression, 1957.

Kant, I. *Grundlegung zur Metaphysic der Sitten.*

Lactantius *The Works of Lactantius,* Edinburgh, T. & T. Clark, 1871, trans. W. Fletcher.

Lecerf, A. *An Introduction to Reformed Dogmatics,* London, Lutterworth, 1949.

Leibniz, G. W. *Theodicy,* London, Routledge & Kegan Paul, 1952, trans. E. M. Huggard.

McCloskey, H. J. *Meta-Ethics and Normative Ethics,* The Hague, Martinus Nijhoff, 1969.

McInerny, R. M. *The Logic of Analogy,* The Hague, Martinus Nijhoff, 1961.

McPherson, T. *The Philosophy of Religion,* London, Van Nostrand, 1965.

McTaggart, J. McT. E. *Some Dogmas of Religion,* London, Edward Arnold, 1930.

Madden, E. H. and Hare, P. H. *Evil and the Concept of God,* Springfield, Charles C. Thomas, 1968.

Mansel, H. L. *Limits of Religious Thought,* London, 4th edition.

Maritain, J. *St. Thomas and the Problem of Evil,* Milwaukee, Marquette, 1942.

Maritain, J. *God and the Permission of Evil,* Milwaukee, Bruce, 1966.

Martin, C. B. *Religious Belief,* Ithaca, Cornell, 1960.

Mascall, E. L. *Existence and Analogy,* London, Longmans, Green & Co., 1949.

Meyer, H. *The Philosophy of St. Thomas Aquinas,* St. Louis, Herder Book Co. 1944, trans. E. Eckhoff.

Mill, J. S. *An Examination of Sir William Hamilton's Philosophy,* London, Longmans, Green, Reader & Dyer, 1878, 5th Edition.

Mill, J. S. *Three Essays on Theism,* London, Longmans, Green, Reader & Dyer, 1874.

Moore, G. E. *Principia Ethica,* Cambridge, C.U.P., 1903.

Niebuhr, Richard *Radical Monotheism and Western Culture,* Lincoln, University of Nebraska, 1960.

Otto, R. *The Idea of the Holy,* London, O.U.P., 1939.

Plantinga, A. *God and Other Minds,* Ithaca, Cornell, 1967.

Plato *Republic.*

Ramsey, I. *Religious Language,* London, S.C.M., 1957.

Ross, W. D. *The Right and the Good,* Oxford, Clarendon, 1930.

Tillich, P. *The Dynamics of Faith,* London, Allen & Unwin, 1957.

ARTICLES

Ahern, M. B. "A Note on the Nature of Evil", *Sophia,* IV, 1965.

Brown, Patterson "Religious Morality", *Mind,* LXXII, 1963.

Findlay, J. N. "Can God's Existence be Disproved?" in *New Essays in Philosophical Theology* ed. A. Flew and A. MacIntyre.

McCloskey, H. J. "God and Evil", *Philosophical Quarterly,* 10, 1960.

McCloskey, H. J. "The Problem of Evil", *Journal of Bible and Religion,* XXX, 1962.

McCloskey, H. J. "Would Any Being Merit Worship?", *Southern Journal of Philosophy,* 2, 1964.

McCloskey, H. J. "Why the Cross?", *Rationalist Annual,* 1965.

Mackie, J. L. "Evil and Omnipotence", *Mind,* LXIV, 1955.

Mackie, J. L. "Theism and Utopia", *Philosophy,* XXXVII, 1962.

McPherson, T. "Religion as the Inexpressible", in *New Essays in Philosophical Theology.*

Niven, W. D. "Good and Evil", in *Encyclopaedia of Religion and Ethics* edited J. Hastings, New York, Charles Scribner's Sons, 1927.

Ramsey, I. "Paradox in Religion", *Aristotelian Society Supplementary Volume,* XXXIII, 1959.

Smart, N. "Omnipotence, Evil and Supermen", *Philosophy,* XXXVI, 1961.

Wisdom, J. "God and Evil", *Mind,* XLIV, 1935.

INDEX OF PROPER NAMES